the butterfly rises

the butterfly rises

one woman's transformation
through the trance channeling of
verna v. yater, ph.d., kevin ryerson, and others

kit tremaine

Blue Dolphin Publishing
1987

Kit Tremaine's poems, "Earth's Aura" and "Into Forever," were originally published
in a poetry anthology entitled "A Four Gathering," Capra Books, 1981.

An edited version of Chapter Two of the book first appeared in the quarterly journal
Life Times Magazine/A Forum For The New Age, 1986.

The quotes from Jeffrey Goodman's book, *We Are The Earthquake Generation,* (A.R.E.
Press, 1978) on pages 207-210 are reprinted with kind permission of the author.

For information, address:
Blue Dolphin Publishing, Inc.
P.O. Box 1908
Nevada City, CA 95959

ISBN: 0-931892-15-5
LCCN: 87-24969

Library of Congress Cataloging-in-Publication Data
Tremaine, Kit, 1907-
        The butterfly rises.

        1. Tremaine, Kit, 1907-   . 2. Spiritualism.
3. Spirit writings.   I. Title.
BF1283.T74A3 1987   133.9'1   87-24969
ISBN 0-931892-15-5

Printed in the United States of America by
Blue Dolphin Press, Inc., Grass Valley, California

9   8   7   6   5   4   3   2

Contents

Introduction

I WAS LYING quietly under the influence of a mild drug waiting to go into the operating room for minor eye surgery and thoughts about butterflies were running around my head. I pondered how the butterfly must first unravel from the bonds of its cocoon and then transform itself from an earthbound caterpillar into the skyborne butterfly. It must then BELIEVE that it can fly. Suddenly it came to me that the image of the butterfly's metamorphosis was appropriate for the title of this book, because in a number of ways the butterfly's evolution mirrors my own progress from earthbound materialist to spiritual seeker.

Through the trance channeling of Verna Yater, I absorbed the words and guidance of my spirit teachers—notably, Indira Latari, a Hindu woman of the nineteenth century, and Chief White Eagle, a Cherokee medicine man of no time and all time. In the course of over three years work, I received astonishingly varied and interesting information and also increased my spiritual knowledge of how best to progress on my own path toward soul growth.

One of the most stunning realizations of my ever-growing awareness is the tragic consequences of our current ways of thinking. What irony it is to reflect on the wars that have been and are presently being fought over the question of whose path to God is the correct one. If, as we believe, God is Love, how can it be that God would differentiate between Buddhist and

Jew, between Muslim and Hindu, Christian and atheist? Why do we fight bloody wars, killing brothers, parents, children and strangers in the curious belief that because others pronounce the name of God differently than we, they are therefore inferior and thus fair game for killing?

It seems to me that we have a long way to go, and I am everlastingly grateful to have been helped along my path by those in the spirit world who have given me of their wisdom. To all who have spoken from "the other side of the veil," my thanks, my blessings, my heartfelt gratitude. On the earthbound side of this great mystery, I could not have written this book without the help of my friend and editor, Steve Diamond, himself a writer and constant source of advice and encouragement, as well as initiator into the esoteric world of the word processor. Thank you, Steve, and ten thousand thanks to Verna for being the talented transmitter of my new wisdom.

Finally, I am aware of the great changes which have occurred in me through spirit information. As I was told at the beginning of my work, it was not being transmitted for myself alone, but to share with others, and I am grateful for the opportunity to be of service in this way. As a result, my entire life orientation is different and my realization of the "why" of my life is quite clear to me now. It is my hope that perhaps the readers of this book will be similarly awakened.

Kit Tremaine
June 1987

Earth's Aura

invisible, untouchable,
encircling our earth
a ring . . .
evolving consciousness
waiting to be tapped
by us who dwell
upon this planet.
what if we
feel it now
already streaming
through our veins,
already firing
all our senses?

what if this is the force
we seek and sleepwalkers
and quiet mystic dreamers
already are the willing acolytes?

perhaps we sense our future
and know there is no time
to lose . . .

—Kit Tremaine

CHAPTER ONE

FROM THERE TO HERE

"INDIRA, WHAT HAPPENS when we die?"

I asked the question of the disembodied spirit teacher with whom I had been conversing through a trance channel for the better part of two years. The question had floated around near the surface of my consciousness, but this was the first time I had put it into words. I imagine that there are few of us who have not wondered about death and its potential aftermath.

"Well," replied Indira, "you have form, particularly as you first leave your own human vehicle, except that you shed the densest portion of yourself, your body."

The speaker was Indira Latari, the spirit of a Hindu woman who had lived in India and died there in 1854. She was speaking through Verna V. Yater, Ph.D., the medium with whom I have been working. Indira did not marry, she told me once, and lived with her father in Jaipur. They were both involved in research, primarily in the fields of religion and philosophy and were, to quote Indira, "privileged people," with ample means at their disposal. It is evident from her speech, her vocabulary, and manner of expressing herself, that she was a woman of education.

When I asked her once how it was that she always came through Verna Yater, she told me that she has dedicated her time on the plane where she now exists, to this channel. "I have been with her since she arrived on your planet," Indira said, "and I will be with her until she departs your plane." She then continued with her explanation of the experience after the death of the physical body:

"You shed this vehicle," she continued, "but you still retain a form which appears identical to that which you have just left at the time of so-called death. After leaving the body, there is an opportunity to evaluate your lifetime. During this evaluation, you see everything that has occurred, and you see how you responded, and what has resulted from the responses. This can sometimes be painful to persons. . . ."

My work with spirit began as a result of a conversation I had with a friend at breakfast one sunny morning. We were in a funky little restaurant near the ocean in Santa Barbara, California, where I have lived for most of my life. My friend Suzanne Riordon, and I had met to discuss the problem of the homeless, but after awhile, the conversation somehow shifted to the subject of mediums and psychic information.

Suzanne and I had been brought together by a sociologist with whom I was working on the homeless problem in Santa Barbara. Being in the habit of walking with my dog along the ocean front, I was daily made aware of the increasing numbers of men and women emerging from the brushy area across the boulevard, shaking their heads, running their fingers through their hair, in an effort to comb out the previous night's snarls.

Some months prior to this conversation, Suzanne had placed an ad in a free throw-away newspaper giving her telephone number and offering to help single parents needing housing. I was impressed not only by the imaginative courage shown by this act, but also because Suzanne, while trying to organize others, was herself a single parent and on welfare at the time. She did however, have an old car, and thus was able to offer transportation to those with none. This diminutive person turned out to be a dynamo. Through a foundation I had established some years earlier, I had agreed to fund Suzanne's program for a few months, and we were discussing this over breakfast when the subject of psychics came up.

"I visited a medium a couple of years ago," Suzanne told me, "and she said I was going to meet a woman who would change my life."

I smiled and replied, "And I'm that woman, aren't I?"

"Yes, you are," she said, "and think of all the others whose lives are going to be changed because of our meeting."

Suzanne went on to elaborate on the subject of psychics. I realized that it had been some time since I myself had sought contact with a medium, but as our conversation on the subject continued, I knew I wanted to seek one out. The trance channel Suzanne had seen was in another city, but she suggested I call the Spiritual Sciences Institute here in Santa Barbara for more information about psychics in this area.

As soon as I reached home I called the Institute, leaving my given name and telephone number. The next morning I was contacted by Verna, a psychic, trance channel, healer and co-founder of the Spiritual Sciences Institute, who gave me an appointment for a morning in the near future. I went a bit nervously, not knowing exactly what to expect, and wondering whether I should have questions prepared in advance, that sort of thing. She proved to be an attractive woman in her early forties, with bright blue eyes and a charming smile, altogether a very appealing woman.

Verna asked me whether I preferred a psychic reading, based on clairvoyance, or a trance channeling session, during which the spirits communicate directly through her. I opted for the latter. It's a little like a cosmic telephone switchboard, where the channel, in this case Verna, acts as the operator to make it possible for the spirit entities to communicate.

After arranging her tape recorder, Verna and I sat facing one another. As I was to find out, Verna always begins her trance channeling by saying a prayer which goes something like this:

"We give thanks to the universe for being brought together here on this day, and we ask for many blessings upon this session. We ask that only the highest information come forth. We ask that all the information that is given be clearly interpreted and understood. We acknowledge that we are constantly surrounded by the forces of light and love and wisdom. We ask also that there be much healing for those most in need of it. We ask that those that be hungry be fed today. We ask that those in despair be given some tangible ray of hope. And in God we trust, Amen.''

Verna then closed her eyes and in a relatively short time, perhaps a minute or two at most, I saw her give a small twitch, then a sigh. Her mouth changed entirely, and as her face muscles began working, Verna took on a different appearance. Another gasp escaped, and I sensed the vibrations in the room changing.

In the time I've worked with the channel, I have come to know that this is a signal indicating that a spirit has entered Verna's consciousness. I have become so familiar with this process, that now I sometimes know which of the entities is about to speak to me, just by the body movements and facial expressions of the channel.

Although I had not had a psychic experience for several years and I admit to a little uncertainty—a few doubts—during my early sessions with spirit, I soon came to know, to know with certainty, that there could be no way Verna was faking the process. She would have to be a consummate actress, with an uncanny knowledge of her clients, their lives, and their problems. And, she would have to *remember* all of it, from one session to the next—and with this realization, my doubts soon fell by the wayside.

I was astonished by the richness of the communications, and grew totally at ease in talking with the different entities which came through the channel. As time passed and I continued working with Verna, I realized that, more often than not, if I brought written questions for Indira, by the time she had finished her little opening discourse (which always followed her greeting to me), she had also answered some if not most of my questions. It is clear to me now that she is so often with me, looking over my shoulder from spirit, and it has become easier for me to ask her help: in finding something which has been missing, for instance, or in enabling me to see clearly the answer to some puzzling or vexatious question.

I have also come to believe that when an idea pops into my head, an idea which may have no apparent connection with any current interest of mine, that in all likelihood it is being suggested to me by one of my spirit friends. It is as if I am being told which direction to take, and what I am to do when I get there. In fact, at times, when I am finding it impossible to reach a decision, I am aware that it isn't the right time yet for the decision, and so I consciously try to slack off from the problem. In attempting to distinguish the ever-so thin line between thoughts which issue from our own consciousness, and those which may have come to us from spirit influence, I now believe one of the indicators may be that the spirit-influenced idea will be surprising, a totally new thought, completely apart from the logical extension of the line one has been pursuing.

"This is Indira, and I am most pleased to be here today," began the softly-modulated voice which issued from Verna's mouth: "I wish first to give you some information and then to permit the opportunity to pose questions if you so desire. . . ."

Indira told me that along with her father, she had studied philosophy and religion, and spent her life researching these subjects. During the course of my first session she stressed that I was not being given this information from spirit for myself alone, but to share with others. Early in our work together, Indira told me that in six months all of this would be second nature to me, referring to the spiritual teachings, and it has turned out to be true.

It was Indira who suggested that I begin to invite friends to my house, that I was to serve as a teacher or facilitator. When I asked what I was to teach, she replied that I should teach what I know. I started doing this some months ago, and it is now well-established among a group of twenty or thirty people that on alternate Saturday afternoons there will be an interesting and enlightening discussion at my house. I think it is safe to say that we all learn a lot from one another at each session. The talk always seems to end up centering on the subject of how to reach the God within. It appears that a growing number of us are increasingly involved in our own ongoing spiritual search and welcome a chance to be part of an informal discussion such as this one. Our discussions are in the Socratic vein, each person contributing or abstaining as they so choose.

This morning before sitting down to write, I heard someone on television speaking about the butterfly, reminding that before it can become a butterfly it must first break the bonds of the cocoon which it has woven about itself. Emerging as a butterfly, it must then *believe* that it can fly. Some time after this, in speaking with Indira about my brother Laurence, she remarked that he had been very useful to me "in unraveling myself." An interesting word for her to use I thought, as unraveling our souls is a wonderful description of our efforts as we travel our spiritual paths.

Since learning that the Greek word for butterfly is *psyche*, and is also the word for soul in that language, I feel that the title for this book was inspired, particularly as it was chosen while I was under the influence of some sort of medication. I was having minor eye surgery, and had been given a tranquilizing pill while waiting to go into the operating room. Thoughts of the butterfly story began running around in my head, and when a nurse entered the room, I asked her to write down some of the ideas, being myself too groggy by then to do it. She obliged me, and when I saw my doctor the day following surgery, he asked me what title I had chosen. I laughed and asked why the question. He told me that during the operation, when I was totally asleep, or in an altered state, I kept asking people to write possible titles down fearing that I would not remember.

This butterfly emerged from her cocoon late in October of 1968, fluttered her wings a few times and flew joyously off to a free life. I had finally developed courage enough to leave my husband and live my own life.

I have learned to believe in the psychic process. I feel sure that those in the spirit world can be contacted, can be conversed with, exactly as with someone still here upon our earth plane.

Because of this belief, my life has opened to undreamed of horizons, and it has helped me to have realizations and experiences which I would never have had without this faith in myself and my ideas, the faith to go forward on this fascinating journey. Many of the things I have wondered about myself have now become clear.

Why, for example, did I build my house just here? Why did I have the sun and the moon carved over my front door? Why is the desert so healing for me, so necessary to my well being? Why am I so moved by its silences, the vastness of its skies? And the sun, pouring down on us, a constant source of healing and energy, why is it so important to me? Why do I feel such a dislike for cold places, finding it hard to go even for a visit? And why am I always drawn to simple people, even primitive customs? As I began to learn of my past lives, some of the answers to these questions and others became clear.

Learning of my past lives, through Indira's channeled information from the Akashic Records—a kind of ethereal cosmic computerbank of personal and planetary information—has strengthened my realization that I am a part of all these things and they of me. In the sense that although we are all unique, we also have many human qualities in common. All of my emotions have been felt by you, in one way or another. All of my doubts, my hesitancies, my uncertainties, they're all yours as well, to experience at some time or another in your lives.

On the material level, my life has been different than most in that I was born into a wealthy family in Patterson, a tiny town, almost village-size, in southwestern Louisiana. Patterson is in what is known as the Atchafalaya Basin, and the Mississippi River has had its eye on that basin for longer than anyone can recall. For years, the Army Corps of Engineers has been fighting the battle to keep the Mississippi from consuming the Atchafalaya Basin. It is rich with crops, sugar cane, truck farming, rice, oil, as well as people and animals, all living productive lives in this pleasant southern environment.

The town of Morgan City is also in the Atchafalaya Basin and some time ago I heard their mayor on television saying that they expected the whole city to disappear if the Mississippi ever gets its way. Morgan City is also the center of Louisiana's huge oil industry, with myriads of oil boats based there, and the equally important, and certainly more colorful, shrimp industry has its home base in that harbor as well.

Patterson is a pleasant little river town, full of tremendous live oak trees of great age and beauty, green lawns and unpretentious houses. I was told that now the town has numerous vacation commuters from New Orleans, doctors, lawyers, and others who maintain houses and spend weekends there, enjoying peace and quiet and excellent fishing. Sounds tempting, doesn't it?

At the time of my birth we lived in Patterson rather than in New Orleans, because of the fact that the largest of my grandfather's cypress mills was situated there. Each of his four sons was supposed to live there and manage the lumber mill for a period of time. Our lives were dominated by the mill whistle which could be heard no matter where you lived in the town, but as it happened the mill was directly adjacent to our house, so it came to us loud and clear. Also loud and clear was the whining shriek of the giant saw, slicing through ancient cypress trees newly brought in from the swamps where they grew. I heard a long time ago that a fully-grown cypress, ready for cutting (if a tree is ever "ready" to be killed), was at least two hundred years old. It hurts me to watch a tree being cut down, but the truth is that if it were not for the fact of all those trees having been destroyed, I wouldn't be sitting at this computer looking out at the hillside beyond the window, enjoying the sight of the gentle slope of the land dotted with olive trees and an occasional piece of sculpture visible through their trunks.

In Patterson our house and that of my grandparents were both on the same piece of land. An ornamental iron picket fence enclosed the property, and when I was last there, I saw that fence still standing although the land is cut up, and the houses demolished. One of them, ours I think, burned down.

Beyond the fenced and developed area where the houses and outbuildings were situated, the land sloped down to the Atchafalaya Bayou, and I loved going there. A part of the time the waterway would be entirely choked with pale lavender flowers. These were water hyacinths, and my grandmother told me that they had been brought back to Louisiana by a woman who had seen them in China and had fallen in love with their pale beauty. How could she have foreseen how they would spread and become a menace to navigation?

My brother, Laurence, was born prematurely, weighing next to nothing, and as my mother had such an easy time with him, she decided to remain in Patterson for my arrival as well. Unfortunately, it wasn't the same with me, as I weighed just under eleven pounds. She used to swear that it was neccesary for one of the maids to walk behind her, as she was struggling up a flight of stairs, to push her along, her balance being so precarious.

Poor mother. That must have seemed to her in retrospect as only the first of the many trials I was to cause her over the years ahead. I remember her once saying to me, something along the lines of, " I simply don't understand why you never agree with me on any subject. After all you *are* my daughter but you don't think at all as I do." Ironically, that was probably one of the few times I *did* agree with her.

At the time of Teddy Roosevelt's presidency, my grandfather had been one of the founders of the Republican party in Louisiana, so it followed that our family was one of staunch conservatives and this in a traditionally Democratic state. But conservatism generally follows accumulation of wealth and not until Huey Long came along did any of the uncles, or my grandfather, support a Democratic candidate.

Harry, my youngest uncle, lived a good deal of the time in Patterson, so his ties with the countryside were strong and he was known up and down the Cajun country as "Mr. Harry." This relationship with the country people was a tremendous boon for Long's campaign as Harry drove his fast racing cars up and down southwest Louisiana talking Huey Long wherever he went.

I met the great Huey at my grandfather's house one night, and it was a pretty astonishing evening. There sat The Kingfish, red face smiling broadly, dining from a lace cloth while seated at my grandmother's right, with servants circling the table and Huey the center of attention. It was fascinating, and Huey, as might be expected, walked away with honors. When I asked my eldest uncle why he was going to throw his support to Long, he replied that he was tired of invariably supporting the losers and wanted to back a winner for a change.

But while I was being brought up in an affluent manner, I secretly longed for an entirely different family life. At one point, a family with seven children bought the house next door to ours and I was in seventh heaven. Imagine, all those little girls to play jacks with, to skate with, to climb trees with! Not to mention the boys, who were ready-made for my brother and the other boys in the neighborhood, and besides, one of them was unbearably attractive to me and I promptly fell in love at the age of ten. That was the kind of family I wanted. I would watch out of my window in the evenings, to see that captivating boy walk past on his way home. What bliss if he did and I was there to see the wonderful creature.

I had an unusual education, never having graduated from any school. Several childhood illnesses kept me at home for periods of time—this being the best way I knew of getting my mother's attention, I now believe—and resulted in my being taught at home by various teachers, governesses, and so on. A year ago, however, to my surprise and great pleasure, I was presented with an honorary Doctorate of Human Services degree from Sierra University for life achievements, and the implication of this honor expresses the manner in which I have tried to live my life.

In New Orleans, where I grew up, most of my friends were rather short on money, in fact few families in that city at that time were wealthy. In an obscure way I felt guilty being rich. It almost seemed as if my grandfather might have been a carpet-bagger, having come into Louisiana from a neighboring state.

Looking back I understand that being the only son of a widowed schoolteacher, having two sisters to help support, he was simply a young man trying to make his way in a world that was upside down after the scarifying war between the states. But perhaps that feeling of my grandfather's having been a kind of carpetbagger made me do odd things as a way of being like my friends.

This same grandfather, having by now accumulated a considerable fortune, had given me during the year of my debut, a snowy white ermine coat, with white fox edging the borders. It was beautiful but it embarrassed me to the extent that when there was a large dinner-dance—a popular way of entertaining then, and frequently held at an indoor-outdoor restaurant in the French Quarter—I always checked my coat in the cloakroom, rather than hang it over the back of my chair as other girls sometimes did.

I well remember one night at such a party, having someone come to tell me that my brother had just been picked up on a drunk driving charge. Somewhat hysterical, I set off with two of our friends for jail and I blush when I try to picture myself that night. Young rich girl, ermine down to the ground, throwing my weight around with the police, telling them that my grandfather was F.B. Williams and they had better open those doors and release my brother, *immediately*. A little on the Scott Fitzgerald side, it seems in retrospect. I have long since forgotten which of our friends I was with, but I can imagine their embarrassment at my presence and their fervent wish that I had not come along. I finally did grow up, although making plenty of mistakes along the way, and still making them.

Although I obviously knew that my family had money, what I really didn't know was where it came from. My father was a sick man for much of his life. He didn't go to an office as my friends' fathers did, and yet we clearly had money to spend. It was considered very bad form in my family to discuss money or anything connected with it, and although it is hard to believe that I never dared to talk to my mother about it, it is the truth. I worried about my father's source of finances, as well as wondered what we would live on when all the money was gone.

And so in the midst of plenty, I had many anxious moments wondering about our futures.

After my first marriage—which occurred when I was just nineteen—money became a serious problem. My first husband was a gambler and his thinking about bills was totally foreign to mine. I would sit at my desk studying the bills, deciding to pay this one such and such an amount, then realizing that if I did that there would be nothing for another that was long past due. I would then throw some of them into the wastebasket as they hadn't been owed for very long, and so on, until I was at my wit's end.

Finally, I thought I had a solution. I drove downtown, went to a loan office I had picked out of the yellow pages, marched myself into the shabby place, and on being shown into the boss's office, I sat down opposite him and explained that I needed to borrow three hundred dollars.

The man at the desk showed no surprise at my request, nor at my appearance, which must have differed markedly from his other clients. He asked me only what collateral I was prepared to put up, and I had to confess that collateral was something I had never heard of. When he explained to me the meaning of collateral, I told him that I didn't have any of those things. After asking me my husband's name, where he worked, my father's name, and was I connected to F.B. Williams, my grandfather, I was allowed to leave the place three hundred dollars richer.

I went home elated and spent the rest of the day paying bills. But I wasn't elated for long. The following morning my father called me in a rage. The loan company had, of course, called him regarding my loan, and his reaction was to storm down and pay it off immediately. I was humiliated. My father and mother were humiliated, and probably my husband was as well, although I'm not sure that I had told him how smart I had been. In retrospect, it seems funny, and I imagine that the man who had made me the loan told that story on occasion and probably had more than a few laughs over it, but at the time I only thought what a good manager I was being.

My first marriage left no bad scars. I was still in my teens when it occurred, and I married my husband mainly to go to bed with him. In those days, casual sex, or even serious sex, with both partners committed to each other but unmarried, wasn't easily indulged in.

Looking back on it, this same reason brought about my second marriage as well. While sex is obviously important to a relationship, there are, as we all know, other aspects to consider. With the exception of sex, however, my second marriage was a disaster before it happened. We steadily grew further and further apart over the years, and though I felt obligated to try harder to make it work since I had already left my first husband, it never had a chance. I have always been a political and social activist, even before I knew the words and their meanings, and I believe one's politics determines how one looks at life. As my husband's main interests were racing and breeding horses, and the activity of the stock market, it was clear that we were not exactly on the same wavelength.

Today, as I write, it is January 20, 1986, and for the first time the nation is celebrating Martin Luther King, Jr.'s birthday as an official national holiday eighteen years after his assassination in Memphis. I can't help being reminded of one Sunday afternoon some years ago when I was still with my husband, here in Santa Barbara.

I had been out, and when I came home in the late afternoon my husband was sitting in the living room with a couple of friends, friends who for me were related to the race track and that was about all. They were drinking martinis and I sat on the sofa by the wife who began telling me a story about not being able to reach a certain restaurant in town with her little granddaughters because the streets were blocked by hundreds of people marching and singing about Martin Luther King, Jr. She was completely disgusted by it, and didn't know why anyone should want to celebrate the birth of Rev. King. I told her that I had been one of the marchers. After a long silence which followed, I asked her what was so objectionable about the slain civil rights leader.

Horrified to know that I was one of those marchers, she said, "He was one of the worst traitors this country has ever known."

I, in turn, was stunned, not having anticipated such a violent outburst. I looked at her and replied, "I feel sorry for people like you. If you will excuse me I have to take my dogs out on the lawn."

I didn't return to the living room until they had left. My husband was annoyed and said I had been rude to his friends, but I replied that it was too difficult for me to sit and chat amiably with such a person and I saw no need to try.

I knew the instant that I left the marriage and began a new life that I'd made the right choice. I had tried it several years earlier, but for one reason or another, I didn't have the necessary strength. When I finally did get free of the psychological constraints under which I'd lived all those years, I discovered almost immediately that the world was full of people just like me, with similar ideas and ideals, likes and dislikes. I even discovered that my political views, which bordered on subversion in my husband's mind, were held by many others who were also concerned with our planet and the future of human life on it.

Although I look back with wonder now at the life I led for so long, I also know that I gave both my husbands a bad time in some ways. Certainly if I had those relationships to live over, I would make changes in my own behavior, as from this distance my mistakes are so easy for me to see. The same holds true for my relationship with my mother, with whom I struggled for years as we worked on our joint karmic problems. I had a great deal for which to forgive her, apparent even to others in the family, but I see now that she also had to do her share of forgiving.

When I found the courage finally to leave my second husband, I told him that if he had ever been willing to let me go, he might have always kept me. This is a lesson of inestimable value, and one which I remember often as it operates in all areas of life. The old cowboy song, "Don't Fence Me In," spoke a universal truth, as far as I'm concerned.

I remember one night while dining with my husband and another couple at a restaurant, being scolded by the other woman because I was attending a writing class for two hours on one morning each week.

To nodding approval by the men, the woman told me that I was being childish, that taking classes was for young people, and that I should be spending my days at the racetrack keeping my husband company. I listened with increasing disbelief to the talk about my duty to my husband, remarking, finally, that I found it ludicrous to have to defend myself for using two hours a week doing something that was important to me, as well as enjoyable.

During the time I was building up to leaving my second husband, friends warned me that there would be periods of loneliness and urged me to reconsider my plans. They told me I'd be better off staying with the situation I knew rather than facing the unknown—but I knew I had to take that step. What I hoped to find in my new life was freedom, freedom from a lifestyle which was increasingly distasteful and difficult for me to live with, and freedom is exactly what I found.

As a woman giving birth to herself, I was now free to have new friends, free to live exactly as I chose. An enormous weight was lifted from my shoulders, and I felt so light and bouyant that I could have danced among the stars.

I rented a small beach house after leaving my husband, and at night I would sometimes stand ankle deep in the warm Pacific waters, looking up at the sky for long periods, and the realization would sweep over me that the universe was mine to enjoy as I wished. Twelve years later, I wrote a poem expressing my feelings at that time. I had torn up many earlier ones, until I finally was able to write what I felt.

> *Into Forever*
>> *toes opening, closing*
>> *clutching wet*
>> *sand beneath*

an ocean flows
and ebbing opens
up my eyes

wriggling in the
watery sand small
phosphorescent things

vaulted, intensely dark
the sky and bright
the whirling stars

each spinning
down its own
accustomed path

and I am one
with ocean sky
and stars

spinning
down my
own

I have often said that I felt as if I'd been born into the wrong family. The money I inherited came to be like a stone around my neck, and it is only in the past ten or twelve years that I have come to terms with it. Eventually, I came to understand the responsibilities of being a steward of money, as well as the importance of using it for the greater good. Some years ago, I set up a foundation and, with my board's guidance I try to fulfill what I believe to be my responsibilities to society. To me it means taking responsibility, on both the spiritual and material planes for what you have been given in this particular incarnation.

I had an interesting turning point not long after my husband and I separated. I was talking one night with a friend while we waited for his wife who was occupied in her room. He asked me, almost idly, if I considered myself to be a "religious" person. I thought for a moment and replied that I guessed that I did, but I had never given the question much thought. I then went on to say, now that he'd asked the question, that I think of myself as a person on a spiritual search, rather than a religious one, as formalized religion has no appeal for me. My friend's question clarified some realizations for me.

As it is with everyone, there have been many influences helping me to open myself to life. One of the most important and ongoing was the five years I spent in Freudian analysis. Although it has become fashionable to scoff at Freud, for me it was a tremendous happening. I twisted and turned, wept and laughed, spent hours in safe intellectual discussions, fearful of revealing too much if I stopped talking, and did all the things traditionally accepted for the analysand. Gradually, I began to come up for air, and years later I am still growing from the experience.

I demonstrated for seven years against the Vietnam War, standing in front of the Santa Barbara Museum of Art with others from twelve noon until one o'clock on a set day every week. The first couple of years were during a period when I had decided for the first and only time in my life to bleach my hair. This gave me the perfect excuse to wear a big hat during the demonstration. I explained to myself that it was to protect my hair, but I knew in my heart that my reason was to protect myself from being seen. I was quite frightened for several reasons, and self conscious as well, not being used to such overt political action, but I really enjoyed the feeling of companionship and solidarity which grew between all of us who stood there.

At this time I was on the Board of Trustees of the Museum of Art, and it was amusing to see some of my colleagues— colleagues *inside* but not outside the building—walk by us with heads averted so as not to see me and another friend who was also one of the trustees. As time went on, however, and Museum personnel changed, a new director and his wife came to stand with us, thus demonstrating a nice example of the changing values of the time.

I have had a few experiences which connected me so sharply with God that I was almost overwhelmed with feeling. One of these occasions was on a bright October day in France. I was driving with my husband and a friend from Paris down to the Dordogne and we had arrived at Chartres where we planned to stop for lunch. It was an hour or so after noon when the three of us went into the cathedral, and as we walked towards the dim recesses of the beautiful old building, a sudden ray of sunshine blazed through one of the stained glass windows on the side of the cathedral. The sight of the misty, dust-laden shaft of light slanting obliquely down from ceiling to floor was so moving to me that I walked away from the others to be alone and take control of my feelings.

A similar experience occurred, again in a cathedral, this time in Oaxaca, Mexico, on the night before Christmas Eve. In Mexico, it is called *La Noche de Los Niños de Dios*, Night of the Children of God. I was with a group of people and together we straggled into the church. It was crammed with children, every seat taken by a child, and up and down the center aisle paraded an elderly beadle, carrying a slender switch which he flicked at any bare legs too close to the aisle.

As we walked in, suddenly, from an unseen choir loft, a single tenor voice rang out. Pure, piercing, transcendent, this voice penetrated my innermost self. Again I cried, again I was overcome by the need to be alone, again I had to leave the others, walking over to a dark corner where I could stand alone until I was in control of myself once more. These two experiences seemed like messages from God, and I feel blessed by the remembrance.

An important influence in my life has been my friendship with the Hopi Indians of Arizona, who truly live by their spiritual beliefs. Every action seems a direct result of these beliefs and the times that I have spent with them at Hopi have been invaluable learning experiences for me. It never ceases to amaze me how much they have to teach us.

The Hopi are known among all Native American tribes as the people of peace and many are entirely committed to the practice of non-violence. They are also people with a wonderful sense of humor and often while I would be staying in their house, early morning visitors might drop in while the family was still involved with coffee. They would all immediately begin speaking in Hopi and I would be left wondering what was the cause for their frequent gales of laughter. I used to tell Fermina that she must be a wonderful storyteller as everyone laughed so appreciatively when she stopped speaking.

I have always felt a strong attachment to the desert, to the Southwest, and to the Native American people and their ways, and when I subsequently learned from Indira about my previous lifetimes spent among the Hopi and other tribes of the Southwest, it all fit together as a natural pattern and progression. I have been under the spell of the desert ever since I went to live in Arizona after my second marriage.

When I began my work in the fall of 1983 with Indira and the spirit of Chief White Eagle, a Cherokee medicine man, who also speaks through Verna Yater, it was easy to see where my connections with Native American culture came from. The following paragraphs are selected from the many pages of transcriptions of the sessions I had with Indira and other spirit entities, and I offer them here as they relate to Native Americans:

INDIRA: There is individual karma and there is group karma, all those interactions that you have had in past lives, their causes and effects. And this is exactly what has occurred, and when you refer to your friends the Hopi, you have had great interactions with them before.

KIT: Yes, I know it's true. There's a wonderful feeling of oneness between us. When I think about the preparation for the future, I think about the Hopi as spiritually advanced people. Their lives are dictated by and interwoven with their spiritual beliefs. It's a twenty-four hour a day practice with them, not just "I'll go to church on Sunday." Whatever they do is done in a spiritual way. And I also think of them as being very pure people, although, like everyone else, they have their human failings. . . .

INDIRA: Well, they have certainly carried the promise forward. There is much of what you would call the guardianship there, much caretaking. You see, these have been cultures that you as a white woman cannot be part of, though they can teach you a great deal.

KIT: My Hopi friends have a lot to teach, no doubt about that. Thomas Banyacya is the spokesman for the traditional Hopi, and as such, he travels the world speaking the Hopi prophecies and the Hopi philosophy. He does indeed cling to the past, following the spiritual beliefs of his people as they have been for perhaps thousands of years. He's also a spokesman for the purity of their nation and their cultural beliefs.

INDIRA: This is a path different from the expression that I used. It is the principle that he is representing which is important. There are, you see, those who believe that the principles apply only to this or that particular culture, but the principles are universal. And this universality is also what has attracted you.

A few years ago, I was travelling through the Southwest with my friend Richard Parker, who, among his numerous other activities, directs my foundation. We were having lunch at a roadside restaurant in a Northern Arizona town and debating whether or not to push on in order to arrive in Albuquerque, our destination, later that night. I suggested that as we had no deadline for arriving in Albuquerque we might detour up to the Hopi reservation to visit my old friend, Thomas Banyacya, and Richard agreed.

I'd known Thomas Banyacya for some time, having first met him here in Santa Barbara. A friend had brought him to meet me when he was on a fundraising trip, thinking I might be interested in helping him. I was subsequently invited to Hopi to visit for one of the dances, and met other members of the family, including Thomas' wife Fermina and his grown children.

When we reached the reservation, Richard and I found Thomas away, but Fermina and their eldest son Tommy were home, and with them a man named John Tomson, a socio-economist/anthropologist from Denver, who was staying on the reservation while working on a project which was designed to bring some economic stability to the Hopi people.

His immediate plan was one involving the gathering of native seeds, from the chaparral growing on the desert on the reservation, packaging the seeds, and training a corps of Hopi to do this work, to help restore the huge amounts of land devastated by the mining and oil interests. This would have brought in a ready cash flow and the Indians would have had the pleasure of being the ones to nurture and restore their sacred land.

A man in his mid-fifties, John was energetic, active, and the unusual development of his upper torso testified to his lifelong love of working with wood, carpentering in general as well as making really fine furniture. An interesting sidelight is that many of his friends shared this enthusiasm which was put to good purpose when they had their shelter for the homeless in Denver. The building which they occupied in the skid row section of that city had a large basement and there the staff set up a carpentry shop where the occupants could work if they chose and could be paid a small stipend for this work.

He was around six feet tall, had fine brown hair, and had been born blind in his right eye, a condition which I wasn't aware of until we had seen each other a time or two. John wore glasses and having always had this handicap didn't seem to be bothered by it. His brown hair fell in an unruly lock over his forehead—a Taurus characteristic, I am told—which somehow gives a man a rather endearing appearance. Endearing he was to me, at any rate, as I rapidly got to the point where my heart jumped when he entered the room.

John was director of a foundation, Catalyst, Inc., which was aptly named, as it described his work well. He was brilliant as a fundraiser, was a good administrator and from what I heard and read after his death, ran the center for the homeless skillfully with a staff of about forty people. While in Boulder, he also put together summer workshops for the Extension Department of the University of Colorado. These projects involved American Indians and consequently he had Indian friends all over the country. He would design the workshops and hire the staff with the help of some of his colleagues at Catalyst.

John and I were to fall in love soon after meeting at Hopi and I was to experience the most joyous few months of my life. After a long life, I was to discover that such a thing as a wonderful relationship between a man and a woman was a reality.

It was Sunday, the year 1982, the season mid-winter, approaching Christmas. John had come up from the reservation to spend the day with Richard and me, before taking a late day flight to Denver to be with friends and family for the holidays. That morning, the three of us had driven out of town in search of a particular dirt road leading off the freeway where we had discovered other, smaller roads, from which we could hike through the beautiful countryside. We never found the particular road we were looking for that day, however, and ended up finally stopping for lunch at a roadside restaurant.

After lunch, when John went to pay the bill and I was alone with Richard, I asked him to please make himself scarce for a couple of hours when we got home, as I intended to proposition John. Richard laughed and agreed to make some excuse to give us some privacy. I wasn't at all sure I would have the courage to do this, but I knew that I wanted to. When we arrived at the house, Richard announced that he was going to a certain bookstore to finish Christmas shopping and would return in time to take John out to the airport for his Denver flight.

Left alone, John and I stood talking in the hall for a few minutes and suddenly I heard myself saying to him, "John, would you like to go to bed with me?"

John had a sweet smile and this smile lit up his face as he answered me gently. "No," he said, "but thank you for asking. It isn't the right time, besides, Richard will be back."

"Oh, I don't think so," I said, "I think he'll be gone for a couple of hours."

We then went into the living room and as we talked I remarked that it surprised me that I wasn't really embarrassed about having propositioned him and been turned down. It seemed as though I was always at ease with John, and this was no exception. I went on saying that I had never done such a thing before and was amazed at myself. As I spoke, the front door opened and in came Richard.

"Sorry, guys, I forgot my wallet," he announced breezily as he went down the hall to his room.

"What did I tell you?" said John.

A day or so after this incident, which was to change my life profoundly, I left to join friends in Arizona for the Christmas holidays. On Christmas morning while I was out 'birding' with my friend Katy Peake, John telephoned me from Denver. I was disappointed to miss his call, but I remember saying to Katy something to the effect that I had a feeling that a new lover was coming into my life. Sure enough the next morning while we were still at the breakfast table in the main house of the ranch, where the only telephone was located, John called again to say that he was returning to Albuquerque sooner than he had planned. My heart skipped a beat or two before I asked if he would be staying with me, and John answered that it was his hope to do so.

Some time later he asked if I had known that we would become lovers when he returned. I said "Of course, didn't you?" and so began the wonderful, magical time we were to experience together.

When John and I first arrived in Santa Barbara, I was unusually touched by the smallest thing he would do for me. No one had ever brought me orange juice in bed before John did. When I came out of the shower the bed was made. He helped both in preparing the meal and cleaning up afterwards, in spite of my protests that it wasn't necessary. He said one day that I would find that he was a very domestically-inclined man. I loved those little acts. One night at a friend's house for dinner, a discussion came up about where my dog would stay when we returned to Arizona, since the friend with whom he had stayed before no longer was willing to have him. John closed the discussion by saying Max would come with us back to the reservation where we would be staying until we got a place in New Mexico. Having him make the decisions made me feel very protected and cherished, a brand new feeling which was most appreciated.

During the time we were together, I was in a state of euphoria. It didn't seem possible to me that it was happening, that we were together, that we loved each other so much, and that our future was so intoxicatingly filled with limitless potential, but it seemed so and I am forever grateful for having had that experience.

We reached Santa Barbara in the early afternoon as John had not wished to arrive at a strange place after dark. While we were sitting outside that evening before supper, enjoying the spectacular view of ocean and offshore islands, I got out of my chair, walked over to a pot of blooming daffodils and picked two or three. John protested, telling me that I was killing the flower. I replied that its life would be over soon, in any event, but he felt that I was wrong in shortening it. That remark has stayed in my memory.

That morning we discussed our immediate future, as it was not feasible to return to the Hopi reservation while the ground was still frozen. John had had a marvelous time plowing one of the main fields where the corn would be planted and it was exciting to him to know that he would be returning to help to plant the corn itself. It was almost like a sacred duty in his mind, as well as the pleasure it would afford him. And in truth it is an honor to be permitted to participate in that planting, for the Hopi look upon that task as worthy of high ceremony. In a very real way the corn is their lifeblood and according to their belief the one who plants the corn must be the one to care for it during its life. It is still planted using the planting stick, holes dug out to a depth of eighteen to twenty-four inches, then several kernels are dropped into each hole. It then becomes the duty of the one who planted the corn to water it, to keep water-stealing weeds away from each plant, and to bring to fruition the crop which it will bear.

We planned on that sunny morning, John shaving, myself sitting on the window sill talking to him, on driving down to Guaymas for a short stay and then going straight back to Arizona. I had been to Guaymas numerous times in the past, but had never driven down and always wanted to do so as I love seeing new country. But it was not to be. By that time the next morning, John was dead and I was numb with grief.

We had had a few friends for dinner and after they left, John and I, with one friend who was spending the night, went out to the hot tub. The water was terribly hot, as I had turned the temperature up that morning, and I couldn't stay in too long. I left the two men soaking in the tub, got into bed and drifted off in a light doze. In a short time I was roused by Jim telling me to come out, that John was not well. Apparently, Jim had gotten out of the water, stretched out on the side, and fallen asleep. He woke up to find John floating lifeless, face down, in the water. Medical friends have told me that extremely hot water can cause a collapse of the whole vascular system, and perhaps that was what had happened. With guests at dinner, more wine was drunk than usual—and perhaps alcohol was the reason. There is a seat which runs all around the inside of the hot tub and I believe that John stepped onto this concrete bench, his foot slipped off the wet concrete, and, losing his balance, he fell forward striking his forehead on the tiled edge of the tub, knocking him out. There was a small cut in the middle of his forehead which might bear out my theory. But regardless of the reasons, he was gone. His spirit was free of his earthly body and I was left stunned with shock and disbelief. I remember that for days afterwards, I would be horrified by the knowledge all over again, as if I had not really assimilated it and kept repeating to myself, "but it is true, it *did* really happen."

With John's end seemingly came my own. He *was* my life at that point, and it seemed to me as if my life also stopped on that dreadful night when I watched as the paramedics brought his body on a stretcher through the bedroom where a few hours earlier there had been only love and joy.

That seemingly idle "coincidence," some months earlier, of deciding to detour and go to the Hopi reservation where I would first cross paths with John was no coincidence, as I now realize, and as a result of it my life was to be changed forever on that early November afternoon. There is no doubt in my mind that I was sent there for the express purpose of meeting John Tomson, a meeting which would result not only in a few weeks of blissful happiness, but would also change the direction of my life, as well as the lives of several of John's friends.

After his spirit had left this plane, it occurred to me that he'd had thoughts about death to perhaps an unusual degree. He commented once that my poetry dealt a great deal with death, but I didn't feel that it did. My poems generally reflect my feelings about nature, which of course contains the end of life as well as its beginning, but almost invariably in my poems I return to the rebirth, the continuation of life.

I now believe that my period of greatest growth came about as a result of his death. I didn't go under, although I was close at times. Instead, I picked myself up at last and slowly started the long climb back to normalcy, gradually becoming stronger along the way. I had help, both on the inner and outer planes, and with that help I not only survived, but found myself squarely on my spiritual path, constantly unwinding more of the bonds of my cocoon.

When I look back and realize that my first visit to Verna Yater came about more or less through my idle curiosity, and the undreamed of events and information which have been given me for my own education and to pass on to others through the medium of this book, I am amazed and grateful. Clearly, I believe in the process of spirit communication, having involved myself in it for so long now, and having had so many voices of spirit speak to me, teach me and give me encouragement. I have been given a great deal of information, including material on subjects which were totally unfamiliar to me. I have also received a lot of encouragement, both on my personal path, and on the work I am to accomplish.

I have lived on this planet in this lifetime since the early part of the century, so it goes without saying that I have been around to see some enormous changes. I have seen what would have been termed miracles become everyday occurrences. I have seen impossible dreams become reality, and I am aware that right now vast horizons are being pushed back daily with results which will undoubtedly strike us as being dazzling and—until we know about them—even impossible.

Consider the law of aerodynamics. Although it was only discovered by man in recent years, it always existed. Mankind hadn't reached the evolutionary stage where such a law could be "realized." Now flying around the sky is commonplace for many of us.

Think of snatching sound waves from the air—radio, television, and telephones. And didn't the majority of us once think the planet was flat? Until one Christopher Columbus came along with a different idea and we found out, thanks to his daring, that it is in truth round.

And who is to say with finality "everyone knows that dead people can't talk?"

How do we know this?

CHAPTER TWO

On Karma, Reincarnation
and God

I AM SITTING OPPOSITE Verna, waiting for her to sink away into
the trance state, a process which never takes long. She has
already given her prayer, her eyes are closed, and soon her
mouth begins working slightly. Her expression changes and she
gives a low gasp. As her head twists to one side, she gives
another, louder gasp and I am aware that a spirit entity has
entered her body and is about to speak.

It is generally Indira who speaks first. I have been working
with Verna now for three years and thoughts of prior sessions
flit through my head. Information comes from Indira so fast,
and sets me thinking so hard about what she's just told me that
often the questions I have brought go unasked. And it has
happened more than once that Indira will begin the session by
answering the questions I've prepared beforehand without my
ever speaking them out loud. Several friends and acquaintances
who've had sessions with Verna have also reported the same
thing happening.

Although it wasn't always so, I now have a clear mental
picture of Indira in my head. One morning I was driving along
Santa Barbara's Butterfly Beach on my way home from town
and stopped to listen to the waves, watch the beach walkers and
smell the sea. Suddenly I saw an East Indian woman standing on
the sand, letting the sea wash over her bare feet. She was small,
slender, her black hair drawn into a knot and she wore a

38

salmon-colored sari. It was worn in the traditional fashion, leaving one brown shoulder bare. She was looking out to sea, giving a wonderfully tranquil impression as she stood quietly on the sand. As a result of that vision, I see her in my mind's eye whenever I'm in a trance session.

"This is Indira," began her familiar voice, "and I am most happy to greet you once again on this day. . ." As in so many of the sessions, Indira offered her thoughts before I asked any questions on a particular topic:

INDIRA: We want to tell you today that like all persons on your earth plane, you have buried deep within you all the mysteries of the world. And this is what all are searching for.

There are many avenues to get at these mysteries, through symbols, through self-searching, and even by looking intently at another person, such as those times when you are giving people the opportunity to look at, and into yourself.

First of all, in the understanding of karma, it is to recognize that each person places him or herself in a particular condition through choice of birth, parents, and the place of destiny. When you come upon the earth plane, there are certain things that you more or less negotiate, that are given to you as your bundle to be taken care of in this round.

There are some that will take care of that whole bundle, and they still can take another. Others will not complete their bundle in this lifetime. It is like children in school. Some finish, will graduate and others not. They will have to go back and repeat the grade once more.

KIT: Indira, since there is this kind of karmic planning, what about the role of free will in our lives?

INDIRA: A person has certain large scopes of his or her existence worked out, but not the details. You always have free will, so you can reject your life plan, or change it at any moment. You will find that often those people who undergo certain reversals, illnesses or other misfortunes are there because their soul is trying to get their attention back on track.

Karma is often not correctly understood on your earth plane. Karma means *all* those interactions that you have, more than simply cause and effect.

Universal law never permits anything to remain unfinished. It is that everything is always taken care of, down to the little commas of life, and so individuals often come together for working out what was not finished before in the previous incarnations when their paths crossed. One person may have had an adverse influence or effect on the other, but balance and completion are the sought-after goals.

The recent death of my daughter Diana, who had suffered from alcoholism for many years, has started a train of thought, so obvious to me now that it has finally penetrated my consciousness, that I am astonished by my own previous lack of perception:

While she was alive, I deplored her life from several angles. I knew of her talents, knew she was capable of constructive living, and since I also know of the great need for service of one form or another, I longed always for her to come to a place where she was ready to do what I hoped she would do.

She never did. But what I was blind to was the fact that of course she was doing what she was meant to do in this round— and that what I thought she should be doing was, to say the least, irrelevant. I was considering her life solely in terms of mine, of my wishes for her.

Diana was working out her own karma exactly as I am doing, exactly as each of us must do. In a session after her death, Indira told me that my daughter would never again have to repeat the terrible cravings of this life just ended. I was happy to hear this, happy to know that this lovely soul is to be spared this particular torture in the future.

I have known many people whose lives appear to me as useless, but I now, finally, realize that it is not up to me to judge this. It would be a great step forward if every parent could be aware of this truth. We would never hear again words such as "In my day. . .," or "when I was a child I had to do such and such. . ." This is not your day. This is a different era, your child is a different entity, working out his/her karma just as you are working out your own.

In the course of my work with Indira, I learned that sometimes the changing or rejecting of your life plan may mean that the lessons you have come into this round to learn will not be learned, but will only be postponed until the next round. When I was in school, I could always fake an English assignment, and get by with it, as with some other subjects on occasion— but mathematics was a different story. There was no way to fake it, if the numbers were not right, they just weren't right, and there wasn't any way to make them seem right.

So, too, with karma, it seems to me—it isn't anything that we can hide or pretend we didn't mean. If we have done it, thought it, or planned it, it is a matter of record, and so inscribed on the Akashic Record. I am not saying that we will be punished for these things, I am saying that from what I have been told and have read, it is we ourselves who evaluate our lives, and so, of necessity, it is we who must return and try to learn our lessons another time. When Indira said that this post-death evaluation can be painful for persons, I replied that I could well believe it.

At another session, I asked Indira about group karma, and how it was that we get caught up in it, whether of the negative or positive kind. I was thinking about the Holocaust, the Africans dying of starvation by the millions, and others throughout history who have together undergone starvation, torture, death.

INDIRA: The first example of group karma comes when you participate in it during a particular lifetime. If you are one who has barbarically hunted heads, for example, then you are part of the group of souls who engaged in that particular activity at that time during a particular lifetime. Then you, along with the others of that period, will come forth to balance it in a subsequent incarnation. Sometimes you will come back into a body at the same time as the group with whom you incarnated previously, although now you might be spread in different places on your planet and not even interchange with one another. But you will still be balancing the events of the earlier incarnations.

That which is experienced in your previous lifetimes does not leave you when you are born into this one. It is always there, carried forth. The most minute skills that you learned in another lifetime are still with you in one way or another. Personality characteristics are brought forward. This is not always understood, because the personality is felt to die when the physical body dies. These are imprinted somewhat on the individual soul. . .

In my mind there is no question that we carry certain patterns over from one life to another, not necessarily sequentially. How else to explain that instant attraction or instant hostility which one person can arouse in another with no apparent reason?

The first time I went out with John Tomson, for example, whom I had met only twice before, I told him that I felt as if there had never been a time when I had not known him. I'm sure we have all felt that way about someone during the course of our lives.

More recently, John's daughter Tamar and I met a couple in Arizona on the Hopi reservation. As we walked out of the dining room at the Hopi Cultural Center, my eyes met those of a woman sitting with her friend in a booth. She smiled slightly, I responded. I stopped and asked her if we knew each other, as it happens from time to time with me that someone whom I have met remembers me while I might not be able to place them. She said no, we hadn't met in the past, but that she liked my outfit, and so she'd smiled as I passed. I thanked her and after a few words turned to her companion, a tall good-looking black man. I knew that the Hopi were expecting a certain dignitary from the United Nations, also black, and so I asked him if he was the man from the U.N. The woman answered my question with a big smile, telling me that her friend, Clarence Robbins, was a social worker, as well as vice-president of the New York City chapter of the Psychotronics Association of America.

I replied that I knew nothing of psychotronics, but that I had been working with a psychic for better than two years, and would like to hear about it. Clarence moved over, saying "Please sit down and join us," which Tamie and I did, and in a few minutes we were all fast friends.

Clarence also had a keen interest in, and knowledge of, crystals. When we parted company, he said that their vacation was over and

*they were leaving for New York that day but that he would be coming
out to California in a few weeks time and would like to stop by Santa
Barbara en route to San Jose and spend a day and night if that would
be convenient for me. I assured him that it would be, and when I asked
what was bringing him to San Jose he replied that he was working
with a man named Marcel Vogel, a renowned authority on crystals in
all of their facets and aspects. Vogel lectures, holds workshops,
demonstrates the power and uses of crystals and although I now know
of his fame, at that time I had not heard of him.*

*Two days before Clarence arrived here in Santa Barbara, my
daughter Katy called to tell me of her first session with Indira. She
was excited by the information which the spirit teacher had conveyed,
and in the middle of our conversation Katy asked me if I had ever
heard of a man named Marcel Vogel. Indira had told Katy that
within eighteen months she would meet and be working with crystals
and a man named Marcel Vogel. One and the same!*

*I told Katy that my new friend would be stopping by the next day
and that if she would like to come to supper the following night, she
would meet a man who was a friend of Marcel Vogel and was on his
way to work with Vogel for a few days and could fill her in on
everything she needed to know. For my part, such so-called "coinci-
dences," such guidance from spirit, have become an accepted part of
my life.*

*What had drawn me to Clarence sitting in that restaurant
booth? The woman's smile, the powerful vibrations from the man? I
don't know, but it does happen all the time, more so as you tune into it.*

INDIRA: In the consideration of group karma, you always
have your own free will, as we have stated, but as you know,
individuals get caught up in group situations every day, posi-
tively and negatively. You hear people say things like, "Well, I
had to do it, so and so made me do it," or, "the circumstances"
made it unavoidable, but it is really because they do not want to
acknowledge that they and they alone, are responsible for their
own actions. The individual must learn to pay attention to her
or his own free will and understand that they must use it.

You see, always there is a patterning in the experiences and existences of each person. This pattern isn't created by someone else, by some force outside of them. It's created by themselves. Now patterns can be altered, but once you set the alteration in motion, that's what you're dealing with. It is important to make individuals aware of this so that they will understand that the patterning is projected onto the future. One of the most important aspects which people don't realize is that it might take a certain number of lifetimes to balance out a particular pattern.

Then, too, there are situations in which the person is given the opportunity and permission to experience and to garner and put together that which is of their very highest experience. Take for example your little musicians. The ones who go to your instruments and immediately know how to play them.

KIT: You mean a gifted young child? A young Mozart?

INDIRA: Correct, but there are others, lesser known, who still have the pattern. What he did was to develop the pattern each time he had the opportunity in order to come closer and closer to the perfection of his chosen patterns. The same applies for any pattern, such as one who is in the pattern of the healing force. Their choice is to develop it to the highest, or just to develop it, but it's still the same pattern at work.

And there are those also who choose never to develop their talents, or their patterns, as Indira says.

KIT: Going back to the subject of our karmic ties and the way different people provide service during their lifetimes— I am one of those who has a compulsion to help others when asked. Right now I have a friend in jail. I funded a lawyer to handle his case. He was sentenced and now I'm being asked to secure another lawyer to review the case. I'll probably do it because of this need I seem to have to help people, but I wonder at times if perhaps my need to help people isn't neurotic in itself.

INDIRA: First it is always to remember that your free will is at work. At times you will come across individuals to whom you owe a debt. I don't mean in the sense that you borrowed money or anything from them. But it might be a debt you owe from another incarnation. Karmic debts can be incurred in many ways. It can be that they saved your life. It can be a simple interrelationship from a single previous existence, or interrelationships that have transpired between you and them over many lifetimes.

Most often when these life-crossings occur, you will be put in the position of choosing whether or not you want to assist. If you don't do it this time, you're going to be given an opportunity to help them in another round in the future.

Note how Indira says we will be given the opportunity to help. Not that we will have to help. This, of course, demonstrates the tremendous part our free will plays in the understanding and resolution of the karmic patterns in our lives.

INDIRA: You must ask yourself in this particular situation, as in others like this one, is there an opportunity to build into this some sort of coming to grips for him, with who he is, and what his karma is along these lines. It isn't alone the providing of assistance to pop himself out of the cellblock so to speak, because on a larger scale there is something more important at work, a principle of life.

Indira's advice regarding my friend reminds me of the old saying that to give a man a fish feeds him for a day, but to teach him to fish will feed him for a lifetime. She then goes on to say:

If you can assist him in opening of himself, for review of his life which will change him, this is probably more important than whether or not you eventually provide the funds that are being requested. You see, if you can reach him on a deeper level, *one which will have profound impact for his future lives to come,* then something special will have been achieved. This is the nature of karmic interaction, karmic balancing.

Taking time to review our lives is a task that very few of us get around to, I suspect.

Speaking for myself I don't remember ever consciously doing this, yet I have done a lot of meditating, a lot of reading and applying what I read, a lot of talking with others whose knowledge and opinions I respect, so I suppose that all this could come under the heading of reviewing my life.

In the understanding of both karma and service, Indira has told me never to feel sorry for any conditions or circumstances in which an individual has placed him or her self. It is necessary for that person to be there, to be in that handicapped body, or to be afflicted in one way or another, just as it is necessary for them to have been born into a male or female body. It is of necessity for their particular growth. Reach out a helping hand if it seems appropriate, but to try to change the particular circumstance is to rob that person of the opportunity to learn the lesson they have set themselves to learn.

Reincarnation being such a controversial subject, I have a great curiosity about how people respond to it. For my part, I have felt it to make perfect sense since I first thought about it in my childhood. What is gained by a few years on this or another planet, taking years to learn even a little of anything, then poof! . . . snuffed out, dust to dust? Without some purpose, of which reincarnation is an integral mainspring, life doesn't make sense to me. Take a few minutes, hours, days, or years, and examine your own thoughts on the subject. Do you think you might return into another body? And what use will you make of it? Unfinished business taken care of? New knowledge, new skills, to share with others in future world service perhaps? Maybe to satisfy some unrealized longings left over from this time around? Who knows?!

I have been told by spirit that we already "know" what our circumstances will be when we return. Your circumstances are not accidental, they have been "chosen" for the most part, by you, even including your parents. At the very least this is an extremely provocative thought, and not always an easy one to believe. But it pays to wrestle around with it a bit.

KIT: Indira, many times people ask about the souls of animals as opposed to humans. Does an animal have a recurring soul? And do they eventually graduate to human consciousness? Or a consciousness even similar to ours?

INDIRA: Animals have what might be described as a type of group consciousness. There is some retention of a memory pattern in their souls, you could say, a memory of the experiences they've had on your earth. But they do not develop into human spirit. Nor can a human spirit retrograde, then to be incarnated in animal form, though many of those on your earth plane often jest about it. The animal world was created to provide a certain kind of love, a certain kind of balance on your earth plane, not unlike the inhabitants of your plant world.

Here I return to the all important question with which I began this book:

KIT: Indira, what happens when we leave this body, when the spirit inside us leaves this plane of existence?

INDIRA: Well, you have form, particularly as you first leave your own human vehicle, except that you are shedding the densest portion of yourself, the body. You shed this, but you still retain a form which appears identical to that which you have just left at the time of so-called death. You would be able to recognize yourself, although this alters somewhat on the spirit plane. But first, when you leave, you are offered an opportunity. Some of this information will vary depending on each individual's specific evolution, so we are giving you a general description of these conditions.

If, for example, an advanced master were to leave the earth plane, he or she would have the opportunity to go very quickly from what appears to be a dense form to a totally different form. But this is more unusual than what takes place as a general rule.

When the soul leaves the physical body, there is still a vibrational form that is in much similarity to that physical form, and if you were to look upon it, you would want to reach out and touch it, just as if you were there in front of your mirror. During a portion of time, and again, this will vary depending on the evolution of the individual, there is given an opportunity for a period of rest when first coming upon our planes (i.e. after leaving the body).

There is given an opportunity to evaluate this lifetime you have just completed. It is of great irony at times, when the individual encounters what has gone before because of the response he or she chose, and because perhaps another response could have been chosen that would have resulted in more growth during that lifetime. But nevertheless, this review on the astral is always given in the form of understanding, not in punishment. Then, for the most part, there is given another period of time in which the individual is able to consider the next direction, a period of blissful rest, called *devachan* in Sanskrit/Buddhist terminology, when he or she is not pressed upon what to do next.

Think back now, on what I wrote a few pages ago about taking time occasionally to review your life. Might save time on the next plane! A work-in-progress report on yourself could change the whole direction you are now going in, if you felt such a change would be good.

INDIRA: When one first leaves the body, he or she is given opportunities for general learning, coaching, you might say. If they have passed over very quickly, they may need more assistance to become aware of the new condition. If they have taken their own lives, for example, or have had certain forms of mental illness as you term it upon your earth plane, they are also given more assistance.

Although the physical plane has been left behind, the mental and emotional are not. And then there comes the decision, ultimately, as to what would be the greatest benefit in form of study, in the consideration and preparation for a return to the physical form. When we say that each item of the earth plane existence is examined, we mean literally each thing that you have done. Now you might say, "Goodness, that would take forever to review."

KIT: Well, it would surely take a long time.

INDIRA: No, time is entirely different here than you are accustomed to upon your earth. But there is sufficient time and energy given to this aspect of the individual's evolution to reflect, to understand how the course of his or her choices during the lifetime have affected their growth. As we have made clear, it is different for each person. And when the decision is made for the returning to a physical existence, there is preparation, planning.

KIT: Who decides this? How is it determined?

INDIRA: Sometimes the person alone, or sometimes with the assistance of teachers and guides on our plane. Because for some persons, they are not in a position enough to decide for themselves. They don't just return to a physical incarnation because they desire to do so. It is accomplished from an evaluation of what could occur to be in the highest soul growth in that individual's cycle.

When I think about my own next round I find myself hesitating. I realize now that what I have to give is much in the form of teaching. When Indira spoke once about what I will do in my next incarnation, I began to understand the pattern of my past lives, too. In most of the ones I have been told about I was involved in some way with disseminating information, from the time of one of my Essene lives, to helping my mate in his task of stewardship in Egypt (this occurred more than once), to gathering the women around me in one of my Hopi rounds after I'd become an elder. We would sit together weaving, making pots, and always I taught in one way or another, though I probably wouldn't have thought of it in terms of the word "teacher." And that is just what I want to continue doing, increasing my skills in each lifetime and thereby serving more and more learners. I am no longer so concerned with details, where, how, and with whom I will be in a future incarnation. I will be where I am meant to be, and doing what I am meant to do just as I am now.

INDIRA: Sometimes individuals incarnate in order to meet with certain persons during the lifetime. They may need to meet with certain *groups* of persons, they may need to meet with them in certain of your countries, or in particular races of people. You already "know" as you would term it, what your circumstances are going to be when you incarnate. You don't by some strange accident fall into the circumstances of your life. You bring these circumstances into the incarnation which you, for the most part, have chosen. Naturally, there are a number of different explanations of this, dependent again on the soul in question and the work which he or she is being reincarnated to accomplish.

Sometimes, they're placing themselves into difficult, or what you would call difficult circumstances of life because, before coming back in, they feel that they have the strength this time to deal with these conditions. But once they arrive they don't have that strength, and they fail their task. Well, it's not permanent failure. They have failed this time but there will be another opportunity given, and another, as needed.

You might ask, "Well, since we have the teachers to help, where are the teachers during this period?"

The teachers cannot take away your individual free will. This can never be permitted. Even when we observe the positive, that the person took a step, small or large, in a positive direction, we still can't involve ourselves, we can't push the person. The teachers or guides, if such be the case, are always present. They don't abandon a person, and they do try to reach them. They try, incidentally, in many ingenious ways, but unless the person is open once the veil has been drawn, they may not be able to reach them.

KIT: What are the ways that spirit teachers or guides try to reach us?

INDIRA: For example, when you suddenly think of something you feel compelled to accomplish. Or perhaps on a particular day, when you pick up your little machine because you feel a need to speak with a certain person. Or you might go to a particular gathering, one, let us say, that you were not originally intending to go to, because there was something you needed to hear at that gathering, and so a gentle influence was impressed upon you. It works in reverse, also, for quite often you will feel the sensation not to attend a particular function, and your "intuition" will prove to be correct.

Sometimes, it can be in the form of putting you in touch with another person who will be present at such and such a gathering which you thought you weren't going to attend in the first place. (As when Richard and I sat over lunch in Arizona, idly discussing whether to hurry on to New Mexico or spend another night en route— and ending up deciding to stop and visit my Hopi friends in Oraibi. It was there that I met John Tomson who was to become the most important person in my life.) And when you go to that particular event, you end up meeting the other person, regardless of the reasons which drew you there. Sometimes, those of us in spirit have to try two, three, or four times in this manner of bringing people together, but we are very patient.

There is much work being done on the spirit plane in concert with others here. We work with other persons and spirits involved, and the teachers often have to influence as many as possible when there is a specific need to bring certain people together, either for a particular function, to produce a product, let us say, or simply to have a vibrational effect on one another's lives.

KIT: I have the feeling, Indira, that all over this planet human consciousness is rising and the intensity of the spiritual search is increasing. When I discuss this with friends, I sometimes hear the reply, "How can you say this? Look at the terrible things that are happening in the world." It is true, and yet I have an inner certainty. I know we are becoming more and more aware of our human potential.

INDIRA: This is true, very much so. But when someone says to you, "Look at the terrible things that are happening in the world," they are often condemning God. But as we have told you before, God permits everything.

KIT: Lately Indira, I seem to be more aware of God, the God-force, and the necessity for recognizing it more than ever. I was at lunch recently with a friend and we were talking about various things. I remarked that at this point in my life I am more open to God than ever before, adding that it had all happened so quickly. Then I laughed and corrected myself, realizing that of course it hasn't happened quickly at all, it's been happening over the course of my whole life.

INDIRA: Well, it's been happening quickly because it is of necessity, not only for you, but others as well, to acknowledge. This will be even more so within the next ten to fifteen years, that more and more individuals will acknowledge the God-force in their lives. Some will acknowledge during the course of their journey, some won't until there is dire stress in their lives, you understand? When there is dire stress on your planet, then even more will ever begrudgingly acknowledge God.

I have entirely altered my feelings about God since working with spirit. Prior to this time in my life, I hadn't given too much thought to God, and when I did it was only in the vaguest way of a kindly, all-powerful father figure, who could grant prayers if it seemed right for them to be granted. And although my prayers often were for others, sometimes for others in general, more often they were for myself.

A few years ago my friend Richard and I spent two weeks at a friend's house in Provence, in the south of France. Our hostess was an old friend and it was during this visit that I became aware of how often and how sweetly she used the word "God." I began trying it out myself, tentatively at first, then with increasing confidence, having always been rather embarrassed by saying the word aloud. Somewhat to my surprise it became easier and easier and now it comes as naturally to my lips as it did then to my friend Denny's.

Now, the God-force which is the Source of All Life is the concept I live with. When Indira talks about vibrations, going ever faster, becoming color, becoming light, becoming sound, becoming at last The Soundless Sound, "and the Soundless Sound is God," it is a concept that I can grasp.

"You see, there are only two basic things that all come upon your earth plane to do," Indira has said, on more than one occasion. "Each individual has a different little piece of the jigsaw puzzle, but the two basic things that you come to do are to learn to know and love self, and to learn to know and love God. All else is really extraneous."

I have pondered those words on numerous occasions since that conversation.

Well, we say, we surely know ourselves, but it's a rather tricky question. Do we know if we act or react for example? Many of us spend our lives reacting to others, what they said or did, not knowing that's what we're doing. Then one day, like a sudden, blinding light, you know that you have had an independent thought. At least that's the way it happened with me. I don't remember the thought itself, but I remember that I knew it wasn't influenced by either my husband or my mother. What a triumph!

And then to love ourselves. It isn't as easy as you might believe, as you ponder on what a good person you are, this way, that way.

Eventually, you start to wonder about the little hidden things that you don't really want anyone to know about. All the meannesses, the lack of self-discipline, lack of true love for our fellow humans— there are quite a few things about ourselves after all that we would prefer not to reveal.

Some years ago I worked at a counseling center and it struck me that most of my clients shared a similar fear: "If they knew what I am really like inside, they'd hate me." I discovered during that time how hard it is for people to really love themselves. It was just as hard for me, believe me, and although I have pretty well come to terms with myself, there are still all too many times when I wonder if I ever will learn the lessons I am here to learn.

Loving God isn't as easy as it sounds, either. For myself it is only in the past few years that I am comfortable even talking about God. Now, God is usually the focus of the alternate Saturdays when friends come here to my home for an afternoon of serious discussion.

INDIRA: There are many ways of getting to know God, and of getting to know the self. It is a lifelong, many lives-long process that not only you, but all people have to make. Always teach that the individual has a direct connection with God. For of this there is not much understanding. There is belief in God, there is a trembling of God, but there is not much knowing of God. Do you understand this?

KIT: I think I understand what you're telling me.

Verna has told me of the time when she was conducting a group trance session, and one man had been selected to be the questioner. At one point, Indira, who was speaking through Verna, asked the man if he believed in God.

"Yes, I do, more or less," the man replied, whereupon everyone fairly fell out of their chairs laughing.

INDIRA: God is like the tremendousness of energy that surrounds everything.

Speak both of God the Father and God the Mother, for it is more than this even. God is neither the father nor the mother, but it is comforting for some to think in these terms. God contains all the energies, God is neither male nor female nor androgenous, even this is in error, for God simply IS. But because it is of comfort to individuals to know what it is like to be cradled by the father, or by the mother, this is at times used as a symbolic explanation to assist people to come into the closeness for themselves.

There has also been much in the way of putting God in a vein of revenge, of, how you say, getting even. But this is erroneous, for there isn't anything like that at all in God. That is, God allows all things, but there is not one iota, not one trace, of what you would call anger in God. Not one, not even one small trace! God does not judge.

KIT: I wouldn't imagine that there would be. I think God must be exactly as has been said, God is Love.

INDIRA: That is correct, but it is so difficult to get it across to some. And they are afraid to ask the loving God for what they need, or for help. Many are afraid to simply pray to this loving God, you see? It is quite fine to call on God's help, for that is calling upon the highest.

But still, you and each person on your earth plane have ultimate responsibility for settling all your own karma, for learning and understanding and growing in this particular manner, and moving forward in your service. But it is not so simplistic or automatic to say you accept God and that's it. You can accept God, but you also have to accept your own responsibility. God created the individual with free will and along with that the opportunities to learn, to struggle, to grow, all of which ultimately result in a shining of the soul.

I began to appreciate the changes in myself when it occurred to me that more and more people were seeking me out. I began doing some serious pondering on the subject of what had made this come about. I still don't really know, although I have some ideas, but rather than try to articulate this new level of positive energies which I began to feel surrounding me, I knew it was important to nurture these developing qualities. And this I work on daily, trying never to lose

*sight of my understanding of our purpose here on this planet—to help
all beings in all ways. "World servers," to quote Indira.*

INDIRA: Sometimes we observe two persons on the earth
plane, each pressing for and trying to explain their own point of
view to the other, but neither one understanding. First of all,
they may not be listening. Secondly, they've both experienced
it differently. It is with some anguish that we observe from here
that there are people who would allow only a single path to
God.

If you were to observe all the ways there are to reach God,
all the branches, all the intricacies, all the individualities, all of
the different manners and aspects of greeting God, you would
be overwhelmed. It is overwhelming to most persons. *There is
no single way to God and that is it!* That would be no richness at
all. And while God has created the many different avenues and
approaches, it is correct to remember that there is only one
place, ultimately, to go.

KIT: Interestingly enough, I had a real example of this just
yesterday. There's a man in my poetry class, a fundamentalist
minister, who likes to write and talk about God and Christ. But
he writes about it in a very abstract way. I lent him a book by the
Sufi poet, Kabir, in which he writes about God, and yet I don't
think he uses the word more than a very few times.

My friend had the book for about a month, then returned
it to me yesterday with a note saying, "Of course you and I, Kit,
look at God entirely differently." He said in his note, "At least
Kabir does write about love, and that is a beginning." And I
thought to myself, he has no idea what Kabir is writing about,
because if Kabir is writing about anything, he is writing about
God, and the way he refers to God is by the word Love. If God
is Love, what's the difference?

INDIRA: What is unfortunate is that there are those like
your acquaintance who will take their own roadblocks and put
them over someone else's path, saying you can't take that path
or you can't take this one. Even some who are seemingly
enlightened will try to do this to others.

It is also unfortunate for those of us on our plane to
observe the aspects in which there are battles fought over the

route to God. One of the most important messages for persons to know is that there is indeed a rich and broad spectrum to life and to knowing God.

KIT: Can you give me more information on the nature of God, or perhaps the form of God, if there is such a thing?

INDIRA: First, it is to realize that the whole universe is held together with sound. *Sound is the glue that holds the universe together.* You've certainly heard the expression that "In the beginning was the Word"? Well, that gives you the signal that it is held together with sound. And the soundless sound is God, you see? *All the frequencies within the universe are contained within that soundless sound we call God.*

When the vibrations speed up, constantly faster, faster, the very speed itself becomes light, and when that happens, when the sound is so rapid that it manifests as light, as color, when that occurs, that soundless sound we just spoke of is God.

Each human being has a particular sound, one that is different from his or her neighbor's, different from those across your ocean or in other parts of your earth plane. It is part of your soul pattern, it has always been, and it will never change.

KIT: Does this have anything to do with the compatibility of souls? Their sounds resonating together?

INDIRA: Yes, it does, though it isn't actually utilized upon your earth plane, but it has to do with vibration.

KIT: It is interesting to me that it often boils down to these seemingly contradictory truths. On the one hand, we're each separate individuals on our own particular paths, following what we think of as a karmic plan, and yet, on the other hand, we are people of free will. These two ideas, forces—if you wish to call them that—seem to be contradictory, and I know a lot of people have difficulty with it. Both things are true, a karmic plan and free will as well. And I think that when we understand this dual principle, we're probably a lot closer to our understanding of God, or the God-force.

INDIRA: In this you are indeed correct.

CHAPTER THREE

The Path of the Channel

AS I SOONED LEARNED, Verna was working as a nationally-recognized planning and research consultant for universities and federal agencies in the mid-'70s, and spirit communication was the furthest thing from her mind. In fact, as she told me during our interviews, "I didn't even know what the word *medium* meant."

That certainly changed when, on June 30, 1977, she had a dramatic reading with an elderly Santa Barbara medium, Rev. George Daisley, an English psychic whom I'd seen some years earlier. And, as the forces would have it, going to the clairvoyant wasn't even Verna's idea in the first place: a woman in her office had just seen George Daisley and insisted that Verna should call for an appointment with him. "I kept thinking that she's got to talk about something else other than this spirit stuff," Verna recalled with a chuckle, "but she wouldn't let go of it, until finally she insisted on making the call for me, right then and there."

Verna returned to her office hoping perhaps someone would talk her out of keeping the appointment, but when she told two co-workers that she was going to see a medium, one woman replied, "Oh, you're going to see George Daisley? He's excellent." The other person had always wanted to have a psychic reading and excitedly asked if she could go with Verna to her session. "So much for being talked out of it," Verna said with a laugh.

"The first thing George did was start telling me about his own beginnings as a medium many years earlier in England," she recalled, "and later I recognized that it was not by chance that he discussed his own development of mediumship on my very first visit, because he was about to bring forth information about my own trance channeling."

Daisley described the presence of Verna's maternal grandmother and it grabbed her attention. He saw her sitting in her very special chair, which no one else was permitted to use. Verna says that not only was there a clear description of her grandmother and her chair, "there were energies present which were soul-connecting, bringing information specifically for me."

Verna had purposely worn plain brown clothes, quite out of character for those of us who know her, none of the jewelry which she normally wears, and said nothing to the medium about herself.

During the reading, she was given verifying information about her two sons, Brad and Greg, and information about herself in previous lifetimes. Daisley also told Verna that Edgar Cayce was standing by her side in spirit, and would do so until the day when her own abilities in healing and in life readings matured.

"At the time," Verna told me, "I didn't know who Edgar Cayce was. I remember writing down 'C-a-s-e-y' during the session when George suggested I read some of his works."

In addition to Cayce, the clairvoyant told Verna about other teachers in spirit who were with her. "My life was suddenly turned around 180 degrees by experiencing the energies present, as well as the information from the reading itself."

At her first session with Daisley, Verna also learned that the "spiritual life is going to be very important to you," and that she was endowed with the ability for "powerful mediumship and healing energies." According to the information, Verna had lived in India as a dancing girl in a temple, and she'd had another existence in northern India in the Himalayas. Perhaps it

was during those lifetimes that Verna connected with Indira
Latari. I once asked Indira about this, how it happened that she
always speaks through Verna Yater, and was told that she,
Indira, had dedicated her existence on the plane she is now on
to Verna, had been with her since her birth on this planet and
would be with her until she leaves it.

Daisley told her on that day back in 1977, that Verna was
going to be an instrument through which to channel messages
from Indira Latari in spirit. And that has certainly proven
prophetic.

"Although I had a lot of sensitivity as a child and an inner
knowing, I wasn't aware of the workings of the psyche in any
way. I had many experiences of knowing during childhood, but
I never questioned them. I never thought of them as separate in
any way from normal existence," Verna says. "I took it more or
less for granted that my ability to know what other people were
thinking was quite common, and when I was a child I couldn't
understand why people lied. I cried quite easily, too, and was
sensitive in many ways which I didn't realize."

As a child, Verna had a facility known as eidetic imagery,
or total visual recall, similar to what is commonly thought of as
a photographic memory. "I assumed everyone had this capabil-
ity, but when it disappeared during puberty, I discovered that it
wasn't common to everyone . . ."

Raised in the rural woods of New Ulm, Minnesota, Verna
had a carefree, barefoot childhood, much of it spent reading,
climbing ancient apple trees, ice skating on the rivers as well as
on a pond behind her home which she considered to be "my
very own." Verna's skating pond reminded me of a friend in
Ireland who is so dedicated to fishing, holding many records
both there and on the Continent, that she has a well stocked
fish pond behind her house and goes out in the long Irish
evenings with her fishing gear to practice and perfect her casting
technique.

Although she would have called it "daydreaming" back
then, Verna frequently left her body in those long ago childhood days. "I continued to work through karmic ties with

those on the other side. And when I would occasionally be interrupted in one of my 'travels,' usually by my mother calling me, I'd return with a jolt."

After her first meeting with the medium, an experience during which tears of recognition were streaming down her face, Verna searched for information on Edgar Cayce, mediumship and metaphysics in general. She had no idea that there were bookstores which specialized in metaphysical literature. When she was finally directed to them, Verna let herself go and literally holed up "with a stack of spiritually-oriented books, wondering where they'd been all my life. Much of what I read explained many of the experiences which I'd been having."

Six weeks later, through a whole series of conditions and circumstances, she found herself returning for another appointment with Daisley, but this time alone.

"The second time, the spirits indicated that they had brought me back to tell me more about myself and the directions my own work would take," Verna told me. During this second session, she learned more of the teachers who would be working with and through her, and the type of healing which would be best for her—i.e. healing related to bones, the spinal column, vision, hearing, mental disturbances, sleep disturbances, and growths within the body.

At a later session, Verna learned of other spirit teachers who would be using her as an instrument for communication, including Chief White Eagle, a Cherokee medicine man whom medium Daisley described as having a "marvelous nose and wearing ivory and big fluffy feathers and a deerskin cover." In addition to information about the past, Verna was told that in the future she was to be an instrument for the energies to come through, for both healing and for transmission of information from spirit.

"Then George suddenly pulled back a bit," Verna told me, "and said he was in the presence of a high adept, Yogananda, who had come to greet me. He described him, his saffron robes and outstretched arms. He told me that Yogananda wanted me to regard him as my friend."

Over the course of the next two years, Verna continued to open and develop her faculties through studying, and sitting long hours in meditation, preparing herself for the service that was to follow. Much of this early preparation was done in concert with her friend and co-founder of the Spiritual Sciences Institute, Barbara Huss, M.S.

Verna is certain that spirit forces were at work in bringing her and Barbara together. She and Barbara now recognize each other as companion souls who have come to do world service. They first met when both were consulting for special education programs but had no realization of the impact they would have on each other. Both are now gifted and accomplished trance channels and healers, continuing to remain open to new vistas to explore.

"I was enrolled in a seminar on dream interpretation in Orange County," Verna said, "and Barbara, whom I did not know well, suggested she would like to take the seminar with me. I did everything I could to discourage her, telling her first that I was leaving early to have dinner with friends in L.A., that I would be staying overnight with other friends, and that it was a small apartment. She said not to worry, she'd come along and bring a sleeping bag. I'm glad she persisted in her desire to go, as this weekend workshop was the beginning of a friendship that was to find its roots in many past life associations. It led us to growth, to questioning, to whole new directions in both of our lives. She shared with me during the conference her searching, and we both have opened and grown as channels since that day.

"Barbara and I spent hundreds of evenings in deep meditation, remaining open to the finer vibrations and permitting our spirit teachers to come closer and closer to us. Finally, one evening, Barbara told me she was sure that one of her teachers was ready to speak through her.

"I went to her home and we sat in deep meditation until suddenly Barbara's oriental guide came through for the very first time. I was so excited I couldn't turn on the tape recorder which we had so carefully planned to use." At the same time Verna's own teachers were painstakingly encouraging her to "let go" and permit them to speak through her.

"Barbara's unceasing dedication to helping and encouraging me were extremely important to my growth as a channel," Verna told me in reflecting on that early period. "It's hard to describe the sensitivity and caring that are so vital to the complete *letting go* that's needed to be a clear channel. Night after night she would feel the sensations of her head being drawn back, and the strong urge to speak—until suddenly one evening, Chief White Eagle broke through with a few words. White Eagle continued to open up the channel and soon Indira and others followed.

"The first physical feelings I experienced," Verna told me, "occurred after many months of work, and it was almost as if someone was walking right through my body. I had lots of sensations in the back of my neck, and a feeling of constant change of vibrations and of energy. I was coached from the other side at the time to use yellow from the solar plexus, and to bring it up through all of the etheric centers."

It was shortly after her opening in this manner that Indira Latari began to come through, followed by other spirits who experimented communicating through Verna. Among those were the spirit of Dr. Fisher, a British physician of the 1850s who is the main spirit guide channeled by the Massachusetts medium Elwood Babbitt. In addition to Dr. Fisher, the spirits of Windsong, a Native American, as well as those of Einstein, Rahotapaman (who lived at the time of Ramses II), the Buddha, the Master Jesus, and a powerful band of fourteen healers and physicians from the spirit realm who include the legendary Brazilian healer Arigo, who left the earth plane suddenly in an automobile accident back in 1971, and his control Dr. Fritz, a German physician, have also been channeled through Verna. The vibrations are noticeably different when each of the spirit teachers enters. With some, there is absolute peace, calm and quiet. The band of healers do not speak frequently through Verna, but often give her information for helping people who come for healing or clearing. In addition to those mentioned, there is an American Indian spirit named Takawa, who guards the property near Colorado Springs where the Institute is building a spiritual retreat center.

Verna was given the information about the development of such a retreat center on April Fool's Day, 1980, during a channeling session with Elwood Babbitt who was then visiting Santa Barbara. From Dr. Fisher, Babbitt's spirit guide, Verna learned that the mountainous property would become a center for learning, research and healing, and ultimately a haven during the time of coming earth changes. To say the least, Verna was temporarily overwhelmed.

"If you were to have taken 1,000 people and selected the five least likely people to develop a retreat center and community, I would have been among those five," Verna said with a laugh. "I relished nothing more than privacy and quiet." Now, however, five years later, it seems to her like the most natural thing in the world to be involved in.

In the early years of Verna's channeling, there was occasional resistance to this work from those around her. One of her colleagues at the time summed it up by saying: "But Verna, you're a scientist, how can you do this?" Her response was that as a scientist, it was incumbent on her to check everything out, all possibilities, and not be limited by narrow philosophies or the status quo.

"More and more it became apparent to me that I could no longer continue with my former career. Friendships changed, priorities shifted. During my transition period of two or three years, I continued to work as a consultant but my real pull and energy was toward my evening explorations and growth in the spiritual realm. Both Barbara and I did a lot of soul searching for proper directions. There came a point when I finally took the plunge into a broader scope of teaching and research and service. In November, 1981, The Spiritual Sciences Institute was officially incorporated, providing a framework in which we could do our work and offer opportunities for people to grow and search spiritually without dogma or a particular set of beliefs."

"Without dogma," Verna says, and this is one of the most important aspects of the teachings of spirit. In the spirit world, the ultimate vision of the God-force is the recognition that although people believe that there are many paths leading to God, in the eyes of

God all paths are the same. God is not dogmatic! The importance lies in the knowledge that to be on your path is what counts.

What tragic irony to reflect on the wars that have been, and are being fought, over the question of whose path is the correct one. If, as we know, God is Love, how could it be that God would differentiate between Buddhist and Jew, between Muslim and Hindu, between Christian and Atheist? How has man fought bloody wars, killing brothers, parents, children, strangers, in the curious belief that because those others pronounce the name of God differently, they are therefore inferior and so fair game for the killing?

One thing spirit talks about is the nature of God and the total impossibility of God "taking revenge," or wishing ill to struggling humanity. When people ask how it is that God permits wars, catastrophes, disasters of any sort, it is because we forget that man makes wars, man creates the opportunities for disasters. All is man's doing, not God's.

The Spiritual Sciences Institute, as I discovered, is designed to support people in their personal and spiritual growth and transformation. Verna and Barbara, and their associates, provide classes, seminars, and individual private work to give people personal experience of altered states of awareness. Individuals are given insights into their own awareness as spiritually rich beings.

As the months passed and turned into years, the channeling experience has changed for Verna, and there is no doubt that it will continue to do so. The vibrations have gotten finer and faster, and the channeling continues to change.

"I seem to experience periodic energy changes within my body," Verna says, "and I will occasionally get a giant rush of energy in the middle of the night."

Among other rearrangements, Verna's need for certain foods changed as she began preparing herself for channeling. She gradually found herself more and more unable to eat meat.

"The subtle bodies and even the physical body becomes more finely-attuned during the process of raising the vibrations," Verna said, "and it desires different foods as a result."

She has also experienced a gradual change in her tolerance of sound levels. "I've been sensitive all my life, but now I prefer quiet almost all of the time. I've noticed that as my trance work developed, my body became more sensitive to places and people, most especially when there are many people gathered at one time."

For my part I have always felt a need for a certain amount of solitude and there is no doubt that since working consistently with Verna and the spirit world, this need in me has grown.

In the years since her channeling began in earnest, Verna has begun to teach the steps of opening up to channel to others. The Institute now offers a professional training program for Trance Channels which includes clearing away of psychic and psychological debris, fear, resistance, and whatever blocks are in the paths of those who are working towards this goal. It also includes helping people to understand the technology of the trance states, and gives coaching to the maximum opening and clarity of each channel. Having supported each other in their own development, Barbara and Verna have recognized the importance of such support to others on the path of the channel.

The following information from Verna gives some specifics on the mechanics of spiritual healing of the kind she and Barbara Huss are now doing.

"In the process of channeling energy, we are often also receiving information for the individual. Information which we receive can come from a universal source or from one of the many healers-in-spirit who work with us.

Sometimes I feel just their hands as they're serving an individual in healing. Sometimes they're giving me information telepathically, for guidance or directions. Sometimes it is their energies that are present, and that is sufficient for what is needed at the moment. They work in groups, rather than alone, as we frequently do upon this earth plane, and, as is needed, they might draw in other groups of spirits for assistance. Basically, they are drawn to be of assistance to others, and that is their sole purpose for being with us."

From the first day that I began working with Verna, almost invariably Chief White Eagle has come through and given his healing sounds. These are extraordinary sounds, both in the manner in which they emanate from Verna's mouth and throat chakra, and for their resonance. Each note comes singly, some fluctuating up and down, others steady, and all seem to come in one long stream of sound, just going on and on out into the atmosphere. The experience is unlike any I have had.

"We work also with the realms of sound," Verna continues, "channeling sounds for particular individuals, depending on their needs. When I say we channel sounds, this comes from the angelic realms. It comes not only through our vocal chords, but through our entire beings. And often these include sounds of instruments as well as those that would come from vocal chords. This serves as an elevation at times, so that people can be lifted out of their bodies to be worked on in their etheric bodies for a more rapid healing process. It is not only to lift them out of their bodies but sometimes just to raise the vibrations for healing purposes. We also use the application of color in our work, and sometimes crystals and other gems for the amplification of energies.

"People occasionally ask if the entities coming through a medium in trance are not part of the channel's personality, their subconscious, so to speak. But let me assure you, they are actual personalities coming through. They're very distinct from our own personalities. Brain waves when in trance are different, as well as computer voice analyses which have been done while channeling. We are transducers of energies, funneling the energy from the universal source to make it usable for each individual. In other words, the energy that's available in the universe has not really been fully measured on this planet because we don't have the equipment at the present time to do it.

"The body, as far as it has been measured up to now, is described as an electromagnetic field. It is actually an electro-spiritual field. The energies are finer and of a wider spectrum than those which have been measured up to the present. One aspect of healing is increasing our capacities of being able to carry certain voltages of this electro-magnetic or electro-spiritual energy. It's the raising of our sensitivity, the raising of our own vibrations, and it's increasing the speed of our own vibrations which serves both in channeling and in healing.

"Like attracts like," is a universal law, so what we expect and what we are, is what occurs. We feel that there are no limits to time and space, and so we can tap into anyone at any time upon this planet. All the records are kept in the finest ether in a source referred to as the Akashic Record, and anyone who raises his or her vibration to that level can tap into those energies.

"There are many ways of raising the vibrations, including utilization of regular meditation, prayer, attitude, expectation, the cleansing of ourselves both mentally and physically, as well as being with other persons who are raising their own vibrations. These are some of the simple steps which can be taken. We've been doing this for many centuries; it isn't something which happens overnight. It may not be a thing for some individuals to be able to do in the preparation of a single lifetime. We've had many lifetimes of doing healing work and as serving as channels of information from the finer realms.

"It is important to realize how the mind is the builder. As we think, so we are. And we draw in our own realities even though we may say, 'Oh, no, I could never have created that,' but we do create. We create every situation and because we have the power to create it, we also have the power to eliminate it. When mind builds the disease or the illness or the accident, mind can also eliminate it. Looking at it a little broader, we can assist each other through the energies, through the thought forces that are present to be utilized, and through the body's own innate knowledge that is absolutely universal and perfect.

"We also carry with us from one lifetime to the next, our thought patterns, both positive and negative. So illnesses can also be built up from previous lifetimes or they can be built up in this lifetime because we are working at the subconscious level of the mind.

"In the course of my work I use a series of very intuitive techniques to assist people in unveiling themselves. Sometimes dramatic clearing and leaps can happen in one session. Usually it happens over a period of time in which we help individuals come into a deeper awareness of their own being. Frequently an individual will come to us and give a lot of verbal ideas about what they think the problem is. I have yet to encounter someone who has a fully-conscious awareness. We're always open to the conversation and the explanations they give. When we help them get to a state of very open awareness, they will frequently come to an immediate realization of what it is that has created their situation, whether it was in this lifetime or another lifetime. At that point, some people need to process. There are people who come into this awareness or its root causes, and it is enough.

"We also ask that they get into a state of prayer and meditation and to have the information come to them that way. This can be done on their own if they're experienced in the meditative arts, or if we help them to experience these techniques in various individual or group sessions, or both.

"The biggest challenge is to enable someone to enter his or her true being, the larger scope, or higher awareness. It is also the most rewarding."

To have been a means for another to become more familiar with their own spirituality is a rewarding thing. It might be that this person would never have even acknowledged the actuality of a spiritual self and it must be very exciting and rewarding for Verna to realize how frequently she has been this avenue of access for others. I know how greatly my own sensitivity has increased since working with spirit and I give my experiences with Verna credit and thanks. Simultaneously, as we each come closer toward our own self-realization, we are that much more able to affirm to others the nature and reality of the enlightenment experience.

CHAPTER FOUR

Light, Sound, and Vibrations

THE POEM *Earth's Aura*, which appears at the beginning of this book, was inspired by Teilhard de Chardin's writing of the "Ring of Consciousness" surrounding this planet, available to all to tap into. This in turn brought me to Carl Jung's concept of the collective unconscious, and subsequently, on being involved in psychic experiences through Verna V. Yater's channeling, to the knowledge of the Akashic Record wherein the entire history of human, planetary and universal life is said to be recorded.

"It is to study the whole subject of vibration, the subject of what you would call light, the subject of color. They are all the same," Indira remarked early on in our conversations. "When you understand this completely, you will understand the workings of the whole universe."

When we discussed it during a trance session, Indira concurred with the idea of the planet herself having an aura and it is more than probable that Teilhard de Chardin was aware of this phenomenon when he wrote about the Ring of Consciousness.

It occurs to me that eventual reports from space (inner or outer) may describe this exact ring of consciousness, planetary aura, or Universal Mind, as Itzhak Bentov calls it in his book, *Stalking The Wild Pendulum*. Maybe if one is far enough away from Planet Earth, this glow, this vibrating light may be visible.

Why not? After all, we are accustomed to the various rings encircling other planets, Saturn, Uranus and their moons as well as doubtless many more unknown to us, so why not imagine ourselves surrounded by glowing, vibrating light, visible from other planets as theirs are to us. Indira confirmed this, but not necessarily the visibility of it.

INDIRA: There is a vibrational ring, a light ring, encircling the planet, just like your own aura. The earth in its aliveness has an aura, just as you in your aliveness also have one. Naturally, they are not identical, but they are made of the same substance. Even the chair you are sitting in has an aura.

KIT: I've never seen an aura, but I'd like to.

INDIRA: It is very simple, really. Permit yourself to drift away a bit, and you will begin to see these auric fields. When I say to drift away a bit, it is to let your mind more or less wander, and you will start to see auras spontaneously. Perhaps at first you will see just a rim of energy waves surrounding the person, but later you will see colors also.

KIT: So, everyone has an aura?

INDIRA: Unless they are just about to depart for the other realm. Then it will go like this, from big to shrivelling, and eventually it is sent to the solar plexus, and then on to the next realm as the soul departs the body. Then there is no aura at all, only a shell. When there is no energy field, the death process is complete.

KIT: Are the soul and the aura one and the same?

INDIRA: No, the aura is an energy field. The soul contains everything, but the aura is the energy field upon the body, moving through and around it.

I was sitting in session with Verna one morning, when I suddenly became aware of her auric field. Around, and extending out from her body was her aura. I can best describe it as a veil of color, not following her outlines exactly, rather undulating gently, as if breathing. Now, looking back, I can't be positive if it was indeed Verna's or that of a spirit also present. Even at the time it could have been hovering just behind her, but at any rate, whether hers, or another's, the yellow green veil remained for a few minutes before

gradually fading from my sight. I regret that I have not seen an aura since that time, but am confident that I will again, hopefully often.
KIT: Indira, would we consider you a discarnate soul?
INDIRA: That is a correct term, but I prefer to consider myself alive in spirit.
Alive in spirit, Indira said, and she stated it with a conviction that left no doubt. I believe that if we had the complete realization of what it means to be alive in spirit, our lives would assume a much greater significance, as would our thoughts and our deeds. . . .

In the preceding chapter, Indira stated that each one of us has a particular sound, and that God is the "soundless sound." Over the course of my work with spirit, Indira in particular discussed the effects of sound, referring occasionally to the healing sounds brought by Chief White Eagle as well as the effects of music on both the physical and psychic bodies.
INDIRA: There are also at times, surrounding each person, what we would call single tones. These are also tones of protection. They are pure, and it is as though there is a clearing, a cleansing along with this. The entire science of sound will again become important within the next ten years, and will be brought forth esoterically and on your earth plane as well.
You see, even when there is silence, there is vibrational sound in action. In your healing work, for example, you may stand in the room of a person who is suffering with a disease, and in silence, you may call in the healing forces, invite them openly to come in, to come closer to him or her at that particular time, so that there will be the drawing in of these particular energies. Of course, God's presence is always there, but when this particular gesture is made it increases the vibrations in the room.
KIT: I'm most interested in what you tell me about sound, Indira, for I've always thought the same thing about light that you say about sound. I see this world in terms of light. Light defines dimension, as well as changes form. It brings out the physical aspects of our planet and gives us a clearer view of what we see.

INDIRA: Well, that is all there is, really. It is light at different frequencies, speeds or vibrations.

KIT: Would you say then that physical life could be defined in terms of electrical energy?

INDIRA: Electrical energy is only one spectrum of life energy. It is one frequency, or minor range of frequency, what you call electricity. But there is a broad range of frequencies in the universe which go on forever, and electricity is just a small band of that. Whenever you invite the healing energies forth to help someone, you are drawing in on both sound and light frequencies.

KIT: I once tuned into that healing power you speak of, Indira. This was some years ago when I was still living with my husband. Our garden was large enough to necessitate a full-time gardener and in the summers he would hire a laborer for a few weeks to go through the woods surrounding the house and garden, cutting brush, piling it in preparation for burning in the rainy season and grubbing out masses of poison oak.

The man he hired that summer was named Luis. He had just come up from Mexico with his eldest son, leaving the rest of his family behind as there was no money for all of them to come to California. Luis and his son had rented a small house in the barrio and shortly after he started his job with us, the house burned to the ground.

Our gardener told us that Luis was so badly burned that it was thought he would be in the hospital for weeks, maybe months, and that he would have to have many skin grafts, and much suffering. Needless to say, I was shocked and saddened by this news. I was leaving for Aspen the following day with friends, to enjoy two weeks of music, but I found that thoughts of Luis and what he was going through back in the hospital in Santa Barbara haunted my mind constantly.

I was determined to try to help him, and kept him in my consciousness a lot. I wasn't really articulating much internally that I remember, just thinking about the man and sending healing energy to him. I must have tuned into something I can only describe as "the right place," and I believe the healing energy that I was sending reached him.

When I got back to Santa Barbara, I was told there'd been a miracle, that Luis had had no pain, and that he was out of the hospital within three days, no skin grafts and no scars, totally contrary to what had been predicted when he was first rushed to the hospital. I felt then as I do now, that I had been guided to tap into . . . what? Universal energy? The-God force? I don't know. That God had permitted me to be the instrument for the healing of this man is probably the best way of describing what occurred. I was awed and tremendously grateful for being able to help in this way.

INDIRA: Well, if you can tune in once, you can do it again and again. And if one can do it, all can do it. It is only to permit yourself, giving deeper and deeper permission to your inner self.

At another session, the subject of sound used during childbirth came up as Indira was telling me about a previous incarnation I had spent in ancient Africa:

INDIRA: Part of what you did during that time was to care for ladies and their babies as they arrived. You were able to take children in your hands and already begin to see how they would function in the future. There weren't a lot of complicated aspects, but it was almost a ceremonial thing, generally seven to ten days after the arrival of a child. You see, during the preparation and actual birth of children, there were certain sounds that would be played. Part of this also was to assist the mother in the birthing process. By this we mean certain sounds and rhythms were used, almost as though there was hypnotic relaxation induced for less pain for the mother. This idea is again being experimented with on your planet. Music can be one of the highest avenues of healing. There will be those that will experiment with technological advances in which music can be felt as well as heard.

KIT: I'm not sure I understand, Indira. You mean music that will be felt as well as heard by resonating through our bodies?

INDIRA: Well, if you wish to express it as a resonation, that is perhaps correct. But it would be more of what you would term a holographic effect, physically speaking.

Your technology on the earth plane is just beginning its experimentation on this, and there will be much utilization of sound in the future. There are some who know how to use these electronic instruments, who know of the effects on the body, but most do not. They are just stumbling along blindly. Of course, many things have been discovered by blindly going along, but at the same time there must be serious experimentation to unlock these secrets.

Vibrations are bombarding us unceasingly. I wonder if that is what happens when a cat waits by a promising-looking gopher hole. Are the cat's whiskers picking up and sifting out the vibrations around it? I daresay that the process is something like that, just as we pick up a sound in our own homes, often knowing instantly its source by the vibrations it has sent us.

It has occurred to me recently that perhaps vibrations, and that "sound which is special to each individual," might result from the continual motion of our blood, coursing through our bodies. As long as we are alive, that motion never comes to a complete stop. Even while we are fast asleep, the blood is circulating, giving off a "hum" of sorts. Can it be that the vibrations created by this movement are the source of our individual "sound?"

On more than one occasion I have gone out to the Humane Society in search of a dog or cat. I can't begin to verbalize that indefinable something which motivates my final choice. It could be an adorable creature, a shaggy dog with hair falling over its eyes, it might wag its tail, lick my hand, do all those endearing things, and plead with big sad eyes—but if it is not the right one for me, I know it, and eventually the animal does, too. It has happened to me that when the vibrations weren't "right," the caged dog or cat in question wouldn't even rise to come to the wire. Referring to that kind of situation, I've remarked that the animal I was interacting with didn't "speak" to me, but what I was recognizing was that its vibrations weren't compatible with mine. I imagine that we've all had similar experiences, with probably similar lack of success in talking/writing about it, because, after all, we're dealing in a realm which is beyond the verbal.

In the process of learning to know oneself, it is vitally important to listen to your own inner voices, to "go along" with the intuitive hunches you undoubtedly have felt and continue to feel. The closer we follow this inner personal path, the more we open to the understanding of ourselves and our lives. To quote Indira, "It is to permit yourselves to believe in your inner voices." It seems to be something most of us find hard to do, but the actuality is that the more you follow your inner voice, your intuition, the more you become in tune with it.

Only yesterday a friend, a well-respected very pragmatic physician, shared an example of this with me. He had been invited to join a group of friends on an adventurous skiing expedition, and had accepted with pleasurable anticipation. My friend is a scientist, a pragmatist, and I believe that this may have been his first experience in trusting his inner voice.

He began by reminding me of a talk we had had sometime in the past on the subject of psychics and spirituality in general. It seems that a few days before the ski weekend he began having an uneasy feeling about the trip, to the point that he finally called the friend who had invited him saying he hoped he could participate next year but that he wouldn't make it this time. And, as it turned out, his decision not to go was right. The first group to go out—it was some unusual way of skiing, involving helicopters if I'm not mistaken—met an avalanche. Two of the men were killed, several others badly injured, and all in all the trip was a shocking tragedy.

When he wondered what the feeling had been, I replied that I would have to call it his intuition, or his inner voice and as it was his initial acceptance of such guidance I suggested that the more we listen to our inner voices, the closer becomes our attunement to them. That was perfectly acceptable to him—but for where I am now in my own development, I would most likely consider it to have been direct "advice" from a spirit guide.

On another level, I am immediately aware when I have irritated someone, or at least I hope I am. If I am also annoyed by the other person, I assume it to be those same mysterious vibrations at work and generally don't make much effort to pursue that particular interaction. It is clear to me how badly drained one can become when interacting with someone on a different level, a contrasting wavelength, so to speak. You make a lot of effort, get nowhere, and finally leave the field exhausted and frustrated.

Another inexplicable and hard to understand phenomenon is how one gets to higher vibratory levels. How *do* we raise our level of consciousness? We explored this subject at a recent Saturday afternoon meeting at my house and although many have had such experiences, I don't recall anyone being able to tell us anything concrete about their efforts.

As I am considerably older than most of the participants in the group, and as I have taken part in many types of exploratory experiences and done more than my share of reading, I have been involved with the subject for quite some time, having struggled along my well worn path for a good many years, and I surely don't have any definitive answers.

Several years ago, William Rainen, a well-known trance channel, would come to Santa Barbara from time to time. He channeled, among others, a lively spirit, a physician who in his last incarnation was a Scotsman named Dr. Peebles. My question to Dr. Peebles was always the same. I wanted to know how I could be sure I was on the right path, as well as doing the thing I was supposed to be doing. What I didn't know was that my path, exactly where I was at that time, *was* the right path and that I was just where I was meant to be at that particular time.

I worried this around repeatedly, and of course Dr. Peebles' answer was always the same: Yes, I was on the right path, and yes, I was doing what I was meant to do. Occasionally someone might point this out to me, that where we are is where we must be at that particular time, but I hadn't reached that point of understanding yet, so I kept on plugging along, asking my question of whomever I thought might have an answer.

I studied, read endless books, attended lectures, seminars, went to hear renowned and not-so-renowned gurus, and without my ever being aware of any transition, I gradually sensed inside myself that I liked the person I was becoming—a real change from my feelings when I first began my serious searching.

Eventually, I began to feel that I could miss a lecture, a book, a meeting, as I found myself needing them less and less. In short, my own inner senses were developing and my consciousness was being raised without my ever being aware of how it was happpening.

I had an experience this morning which I believe I would not have had two or three years ago. I went first to the grocery store, and while looking for something along a counter heard the usually silent clerk marking merchandise at an adjacent counter say in a low tone, "Life is certainly interesting."

I was really startled. I hardly knew this man, was not sure even of his name, as he had been working there for a relatively short time, but it was clear that his remark was intended for me. It seemed such a surprising thing to hear in the middle of the morning while grocery shopping.

"Yes, life certainly is," I agreed, and then asked what had been happening lately in his life for him to make the comment.

"I've been seeking the Lord," he replied, to which I answered that I guessed we all were. "I've found Him," he said, "and now I'm getting revelations all the time."

We discussed the subject briefly, and although I knew intuitively that our paths to God were not the same, I also knew that while the *way* to spiritual awareness is as varied as the number of individual seekers, the fact of being aware of the search is the important consideration, and this man obviously was on his own path and aware of it.

At this store, it is almost impossible to carry your own groceries to your car and sure enough, in a few minutes he appeared with my two big bags. He put them in the trunk, and thanked me for sharing with him. I was touched, as it was my feeling that he was the one doing the sharing and as he is a very shy man, I felt complimented that something in me inspired him to open up. The thought also crossed my mind that had my vibrations not been raised, that little encounter might not have taken place.

I then drove to town for a chiropractic treatment and was greeted at the desk by Kate, the beautiful receptionist, who told me I had been in her dream the previous night. Naturally, I asked to hear the dream. Kate said it had been a brief vignette, but very vivid. She thought we had been standing just where we were then in the office, she on one side of the counter and I on the other. I had said to her, "Kate, there are tremendous angels standing around you. They are very beautiful and they are *your* guardian angels." We had a little talk about guardian angels after which I thanked her for making me the bearer of such a beautiful message. Again I felt complimented, and again I felt as if I would not have had the experience a few years ago.

If it seems an oversimplification to say that we are always just where we are meant to be on our life journey, an explanation that makes sense to me is that each time we reincarnate, we do so with another "bundle of lessons to be learned," to quote Indira. Or to put it another way, we come in with another set of problems which we must solve, hurdles to overcome, the point being that until we have coped with that particular problem or lesson or hurdle we are stuck there. We cannot go on any further until that lesson has been learned. So it follows, in my thinking, that wherever we are is where we are meant to be at that particular time.

CHAPTER FIVE

Past Lives

THE SUBJECT OF PAST LIVES, yours or mine, is a curious one. When it arises, as it does more and more these days, it always interests me to see how people react and respond.

A friend told me recently, for example, that he didn't believe in reincarnation, but about ten minutes later said he felt sure he'd experienced a previous lifetime in Russia. When I asked how that was possible since he didn't believe in reincarnation, he only shrugged and smiled, giving me no answer.

I have known this man for a few years and am familiar with his poetry and his painting, both of which are excellent. In writing poetry he is obsessed with Russia, the Russian people, their history, their culture, and so on. A few months ago I saw an exhibition of his painting which was so similar to the skillfully-executed Russian iconographic work that my own feeling about him is that he must have had numerous rounds in Russia.

By taking accounts of my past lives seriously, I began to understand a great deal more about myself—and getting to know ourselves, as Indira has said, is one of our primary tasks in each lifetime. With this self-understanding, we begin our next task: to love ourselves.

In spite of the sad fact that many of us go through our lives with a pitifully low self-esteem, I believe that self-searching, meditation, and self-knowledge, will uncover areas which we may never have previously explored. Self-examination turns up facts which reveal, even to our own self-doubting selves, how many good qualities have remained buried all our lives. I wish each of us could acknowledge these facts, rejoice in them, and, in the new self-assurance we would have, we could realize that we have value not only for ourselves, but for others as well.

When I am given information from Indira on my past lives, my mind flies immediately to those places I am hearing about. With very few exceptions they are always areas where I am comfortable, where I feel at home. I think of the south of France, of Italy, Greece, North Africa, all the Mediterranean area, and of course the deserts of the North American continent. I know of very few past lives spent in cold countries—and in this life, I've always been aware that I am a person needing warmth and pleasant climates.

I know also that I need space to feel truly myself. Cities trap my spirit, frighten me a bit as well, and all of the high-tech culture associated with large urban areas today, plus the noise, the crowds, all of these features make city life a hardship for me. I prefer being with people of simple tastes, living in what we, with our complex culture, would consider primitive ways, and I hope never to have another meal in a pretentious restaurant with rich food smothered in richer sauces.

I remember so well my brother's remark on the occasion of his first visit to Arizona, where I was living at the time in a pleasant house on the desert: "Well, this is fine for you and Warren," said Laurence, "but not for me. I need the sidewalks. I am *urban*." As he went on about his need for city life, I looked out of one of the large windows at Superstition Mountain, a good sixty miles away, and to the high range some ninety or so miles in another direction, sighing with pleasure. I knew what I wanted, in fact *needed*, and now I had it. This was some years ago, and there was literally nothing to interfere with my seeing those far distances, no smog, no buildings—only clean air and miles and miles of desert. That was Scottsdale then. It is different today.

When I think of the great city of London, I see none of its greatness, its historical treasures, its ancient reminders of past glories. No, none of these come to my mind: in a city of massive, grey stone buildings, I see only flower boxes below the windows of the more elegant of these buildings in the more elegant parts of town. Flower boxes built right on to the structure itself and filled with dancing color—bright, irresistible, and for me a symbol of courageous effrontery for daring to exist in such an inhospitable atmosphere. It makes me want to reach up to where they bloom, well out of the reach of passing romantic strangers, and pat each one. I love them for being there, and for reminding me that beauty still exists.

In my work with Indira and other spirits speaking through Verna, I have learned of more than twenty previous lifetimes I've experienced. Knowing about my other incarnations has helped me see patterns in myself, in my choice of life experiences this time around. Some of these patterns have changed, some by my conscious actions or thoughts, and some will no doubt continue on into the future as it seems clear to me that we do carry over certain of our patterns along with each transition, karmic blueprints you might say, indicating the areas we will need to work on.

Imagine if you were to see a panorama of your lifetimes spread out before you as if on an extremely wide screen, or perhaps in a hologram. These existences would seem almost like garments of different kinds on a very long clothing rack, garments which you have worn at one time or another. You, standing back from these animated lifetime scenarios, encompass them all.

I have lived as a woman, and I have lived as a man. I have lived in bodies of red-skinned people, black, yellow, and white people. I have lived in pleasure, and in pain. Remembering these lifetimes, through the crystallized information I have received from spirit, has expanded my sense of belonging to everything, to all people and to all life forms.

I recently had an unusual happening in New Mexico. I was in a shop where artifacts of Native Americans were sold, and as I waited for the proprietor to sum up my bill, having bought two or three things, she suddenly walked over to a case, took from it an arrowhead, and came back to me. Handing me the arrowhead, she said, "For some reason I want to give you a present. I don't really know why, but please take this." Was it a past life connection? I have to think so. What would you say? I have experienced death many times and in many different circumstances. I have lived and died in dire poverty, and in the comfort of plenty. I have had mates with whom I was in great harmony, not only spiritually but in all ways, just as I have had mates who were burdensome, psychic and emotional millstones around my neck. All of them were lessons for me—as I was, of course for them.

We've all had déjà vu feelings, the sensation of having been here before, or the experience of meeting someone—whether one who attracts you or one who puts you off—and the feeling as if you've known them all your life. Now, with the knowledge of some of my past lives—three times as an Essene in a spiritual community on the desert near the Dead Sea, both prior to and after the birth of Christ, an Egyptian in the time of Ramses II, a Hopi and other Native American incarnations in the arid deserts of the southwest to name a few, my previously unexplained attraction to these places has become clear to me, as well as my feelings of kinship and closeness with certain people.

I was astonished when Indira told me that I had lived one life at the court of a flamboyant French king, as I could imagine fewer places, fewer environments, where I would feel less at home. But as she told me of that French lifetime—I was a trusted person in the hierarchy of the court, with complete charge over who could or couldn't have an audience with the king, and that my authority had extended to the distribution and receiving of wines as well as many other gifts and bribes—I began to sense a familiarity with the parameters and conditions of life which my spirit teacher was describing. According to Indira, I took advantage of my situation and abused my privileges enormously, making a considerable fortune in the process. In learning of that lifetime, I thought I might have hit upon an explanation of why I've been surrounded in this life with close friends and family members who were alcohol abusers. And although it didn't sound like a lifetime I would have chosen for myself, the more I pondered it, the more I realized that it did fit in with and reflected a pattern of my learning experiences.

Although I believed that I would never have felt comfortable as an official at the royal French court, my life before my husband and I were separated had some similarities to such a life. Having been born into a wealthy New Orleans family, I grew up in a world of parties, where social events were of primary importance. Cocktails before dinner were a matter of course with my parents and their friends, summers in Europe, all the luxuries that a privileged life brings, these were normal for me. On top of it all, I was chosen Queen of the Carnival the year I was eighteen. I was being "brought out" by my parents, and I must confess that it was a very exciting and special Mardi Gras for me. I loved the fact that hundreds of thousands of people were crowding the streets below where I sat on the balcony of an exclusive men's club, knowing they were there to see me and the members of my court. I glittered in my heavily bejeweled white satin gown, a copy of the one worn by Napoleon's queen Josephine, at her coronation, and suffered hour after hour the uncomfortable crown, while waving my scepter in what I hoped was a regal manner. I would be lying if I said it wasn't fun. It was. Fun, exciting, and heady, although now it seems as foreign to me as if it had never happened.

One of the problems of that night—burdened as I was by both my gown with its train, plus the six-foot long foot train of gold cloth suspended from my shoulders—was coping with the logistics of going to the bathroom. Two friends had to be with me, and it can be imagined that it wasn't easy for all of us to crowd into the small toilet in the dressing room at the ballroom. I remember the incident vividly and how we all laughed so hard at the ludicrousness of the situation.

But the ironic truth is that I never felt at home in that environment. I felt guilty, as a matter of fact, as many of the rich do, and it was many long years before I finally came to terms with the wealth I had inherited. Although I had been giving the greater part of my annual income to my foundation for some years, it took me a long time to be comfortable with my wealth. I realized at long last, that I was one of the right people to have the money as I was learning constantly how best to use it. I have never ceased working to increase my knowledge on this subject.

I now believe that our past lives form certain patterns, like those of a well-worked karmic quilt. The individual lifetimes are like so many pieces of interconnected cloth, each piece of a different color, each with its own pattern, some matching, some contrasting, and yet together they make up the whole quilt. In looking over the index of my past lives from more than nine hundred pages of transcripts of conversations with Indira and other spirits, I find several recurring events which are also reflected in many of my experiences in this lifetime. Indira spoke to me on several occasions about this kind of karmic patterning and how it affects our unfoldment:

INDIRA: There is always patterning in the individual existence and experience. This pattern isn't created by someone else, you understand, it is created by each individual for him or herself. The patterns can be altered, but once you set in motion a particular pattern, that is what you're dealing with. That is why you set the pattern in motion for projecting way beyond a particular lifetime. If you could also teach that to individuals, that they will come into the realization that *the patterning is projected onto the future*, it would be of tremendous benefit. For these patterns can and do take lifetimes to balance.

Then, too, it takes a certain number of lives in which there is simply certain expressions of service done. There are sometimes certain patterns of life in which the person is given the opportunity and the permission to experience and garner and put together that which is of their very highest experience, see?

KIT: Yes, I believe that must be the case.

INDIRA: And still there is free will within the pattern itself, to do or not do as the person so choses.

Specifically, I have had several incarnations where I was involved in the stewardship of property, land, buildings, animals, or I was the mate of someone so involved and assisted him as both consort and counsel. In this lifetime, I have built several houses on different parts of the planet and have always been passionate in my love for the land, its magic and its beauty.

I have always had dogs and cats and during my second marriage, was involved with breeding and racing thoroughbred horses. To my way of seeing it, that could be a recurrence of a past-life pattern, just as it might be for a person who in earlier lifetimes had always been involved with grains, growing them, using them in different ways, milling them, and this time around he might be a commodities broker on Wall Street.

My love for, and my bits and pieces of knowledge of both architecture and archaelogy are definitely a recurring pattern from my former lives. At one of my sessions during the first year of my investigations into the spirit world, Indira told me of a lifetime in Egypt in which my mate was an architect to whom I gave both love and support and for whom I was a consistent helpmate:

INDIRA: You were in Egypt in a lady's body, living by the River Nile. You were in much attractiveness. It was a time of some privilege and you had many to assist you. There was also much responsibility associated with the privilege. Your mate was involved in architecture. He understood architecture as though he had done it throughout the ages, which indeed he had. But in your own innate self you also understood, although you have never had the training that he had. You are not going to go about studying architecture, but you will come into opportunities in which to informally assist some that will be searching for things they seem to remember from some distant past.

During that round there was much prayer that took place. Your mate was extremely occupied in this and was most highly looked upon as to how to place the various structures to greatest advantage for this happening. There were certain times of day when there would be the congregating of whoever was in the household or in the courtyard. That would be time for prayer, short at times, but always sacred. You will find again that you will turn to this, and others around you also.

KIT: Although I have been told before about past Egyptian lives, I have never been greatly drawn to ancient Egyptian culture. But when you speak of playing in the rushes along the river Nile, I visualize it immediately. All my life rivers and the grasses and reeds growing in and near them have moved me greatly. I have photographed them in different countries and in differing circumstances. As it happens, I have built six or seven houses in this round and have often said that perhaps in my next round I will study architecture.

INDIRA: Well, I don't know about that. You can just use it at this particular time but the memories are all there because you've had the association.

In a subsequent discussion with my friend and editor, Steve Diamond, he suggested that this Egyptian architect and past life mate of mine seemed to fit the personality of my close friend, Paul Soderburg. An architect as well as a psychotherapist who wears both hats with ease, Paul designed the house I now live in. And, by coincidence—as they say—I bought a house as an investment a few years ago and it turned out that he had been the architect for that house, as well.

In his role as therapist, Paul has helped me through many rough places in my life, including the terrible winter after losing John. We worked together at a counseling center here in Santa Barbara for some years, and gradually over the years we have come to love and respect each other very much. The more I thought about it, the more I realized that Paul fit the description of that close friend and mate of earlier lifetimes. When I went for another session with spirit, Indira confirmed my realization, adding that Paul and I had incarnated together more than once:

INDIRA: This gentleman has been together with you in numbers of lives, not only in closeness, but together with you on the search, in aspects of friendship. In the particular lifetime upon the Nile, the understanding was not only building on the earth plane, but in the understanding that all of the universe is in the form of geometric blocks, theoretical forms that are awash in the universe. This gentleman understood that quite well during that time and used this knowledge as a portion of the principles he employed in his building work.

Your mate was a master builder who understood the use of trees and certain grasses, using from nature to provide shelter. There were widely-used stones at the time to hold in the warmth of Mother Earth, so as to absorb the heat for the entire home. There was also the use of stones as portions of beauty of what was created. In this particular regard you would give many suggestions of how to use the stones in beauty. You designed—verbally, through your ideas—courtyards and areas around the buildings under construction by the mate. It created what you would term a peacefulness, quietude.

KIT: Paul and I have many of the same things in common, our liking certain poets better than others; for example, many elements of design and art, ideological similarities, people, ways of looking at the world, a hundred things, as well as an enjoyment of one another's company.

INDIRA: We want to tell you something. It's always a clue—at times you do not have to have spent many lifetimes with someone in order to come into such knowingness. Because it will happen very quickly, the bonding or knowing. But at other times, you will find that indeed there have been numbers of sojourns together with another person or persons.

There has never been any doubt in my mind about karmic ties with certain people in my present lifetime. When I have asked Indira about this, the reply has always been affirmative followed by her giving me some of the details of past life experiences. It happens that my closest friendships have generally been with men and quite recently I have been requesting past life information on them.

KIT: Indira, I'd like to ask you about my friend Daniel Lentz, a musician and composer. Have we incarnated together?

INDIRA: Where is this person located, please?

KIT: He lives in Los Angeles, and part time here in Santa Barbara. We've worked together over the years, and he has set many of the poems I've written to music. He's a very gifted composer.

INDIRA: We're checking on his vibrations. (Here, she paused.) This gentleman has some interesting opportunities left in this lifetime if he wants to take advantage of them. That isn't what you asked me, but at any rate, he has the opportunity to create—how would you call it?—a shift in music. Every several centuries, there are major shifts or changes. Yes, there are always waves of outer things that occur in your musical forms. This gentleman has the actual opportunity, if he wishes, to create shifts, shifts in rhythm, shifts in what you call the structural aspects of music.

He understands within himself the music of our own country (*India*). He has lived there, and some of this is a shift which would be beneficial, that would be helpful in the scales of twelve. No explanation given unto this, but that it is a prime opportunity for him. He has had other patterns as a musician, as you have also. Not so much in what you call performing musicians, as what you would call what he is doing now. For you have not been so much performing musicians, but more so in the understanding of many different kinds of musical instruments.

He has been more so in aspects in other rounds also in which he has used them in what you would call a more public fashion. But you have understood them very well, and again, in your own heart of hearts, you understand them. You are not particularly interested in utilizing them in this lifetime and that is not what you have personally come here for. But they are all there in the understanding, and in your ears as you now listen to certain music, you simply let it flow by because it isn't quite correct. And there are many forms of those musical shifts that are occurring right now.

During his time in India, this man had much knowledge of how to influence animals through music, how to influence persons, and he has used a lot of reed instruments, also small stringed instruments, very deeply and profoundly. This gentleman can still develop manifold in this particular round.

During one of his incarnations in northern India, you were well known unto him, as fellow musician and friend, both in masculine bodies of expression. When I say "fellow musician" it was not as in your modern day in which you came together in groups as musicians, but here each did of their own, and their own growth and understanding. A form of simplicity, yes? But sometimes, with a single note there was a bird that would respond immediately to that single note. With another two notes, there would be the cobra which would respond. But all this was done principally by the individual, not in groups. This gentleman friend of yours understands perfectly the singleness of notes of music, of rhythm forms and if he uses only the single note, and the twelve tone scale, he has this opportunity to completely change the course of music.

KIT: But he writes very complex music.

INDIRA: True, but he understands the simplicity. He hears the writing on the inside, you understand? And so, he has the opportunity, if he wants to take advantage of it, to assist in the shift of the music.

When I played the tape for Dan the following day, his expression was almost ludicrous. He said he couldn't believe what he was hearing! Then told me that what Indira has said that he must do is exactly how he is writing now. Dan went out to his car and brought in a sheet of music to show me. He had even written a note to himself at the bottom of one sheet to remind himself to continue writing in that exact mode of the single note—not to add another note—which is an unusual mode, to say the least!

The next time he was here I remarked that I had been re-reading the transcription of the tape and noticed that Indira had said that in one of his lives in northern India he composed using reeds and small stringed instruments. I was captivated by the sound of this and asked if he had ever done it, or was considering it. Again it turned out that he was doing exactly that. A short time later the pianist he is working with came by, and when Dan asked him to tell me how they were working just at that time, he replied, of course, that they were using reeds and stringed instruments. What else?

Dan tells me now that he had been thinking that my conversations with spirit were a little bit crazy all this time, but you can imagine that he is now a believer in the psychic process.

On another occasion, I asked Indira about Richard Parker, the director of my foundation who is also my close friend:

KIT: Have I shared other incarnations with my friend Richard, who is so important in my life in so many ways?

INDIRA: Yes, he has been a guardian to you a number of times.

KIT: He's a little like that now. In a very real way, he stands between me and the world, takes things off my shoulders and spares me numerous burdensome things.

INDIRA: He has been an actual guard, one who protects. There have been times in former rounds where such a person was needed to stand at the gate, or even at the door to your own room.

KIT: I am sure that if I needed a guard like that now, Richard would be there.

On the night of John's death, I left a message on Richard's answering machine in San Francisco telling him the dreadful news. He called me back about two thirty in the morning, wanting to know the message as I had been sobbing so hard he couldn't understand me.

When I told him he only said, "I'll be there right away," and of course he was, early the next morning. I can never forget that.

Friends! What glorious blessings they are.

As I've said earlier, when you initially embark on this kind of spiritual inquiry through a channel or medium, there are occasionally sneaky little doubts and wonderings that creep in. I would like to point out that at the time, Verna knew very little about me, nothing about my long-standing interest in the desert and specifically my interest in and love for primitive pottery. When I learned from the spirit of Chief White Eagle and from Indira about various lifetimes I'd experienced as a Native American, Verna did not know of my involvement with the Hopi and other Native American people, whom I number among my friends and fellow travelers on this planet.

CHIEF WHITE EAGLE: I have chosen to speak first today. I wish to tell you of some of your Indian heritage and your experiences as one of our people. You will feel much comfort in this and also much excitement of the soul. You have been in the expression of man and woman in about equal numbers of lifetimes, and so you will find yourself being able to relate to the masculine aspect very well. You relate to the power and you relate to the strength that is there in that aspect.

KIT: That's true.

CHIEF WHITE EAGLE: Be acknowledging that this is so, that learning both expressions of the feminine, of the nurturing, and also of the strength and the power of the masculine, have assisted you in your growth. All are necessary. All will be integrated for you within this particular lifetime.

You have experienced being a potter in many other lives. You have known how it is to take the clay and to move it in your hands to make bowls and other objects. It was not only for decorative purposes that you created these objects but also for utility.

In the Arizona land there are several locations where pottery made by you is still buried. In the stretch of desert between what you call the City of Angels and that Arizona land, there is buried some of your pottery beneath a sunken lake. It is not necessary to dig beneath the area for it is not so much in the value of what would be found, but more for your own knowledge that much of what was made there was of pinks and grays and you will again be drawn to these colors. These colors were much utilized at that time.

I love pottery and I never see wet clay without wanting to take it into my hands and play with it. When I was a child in New Orleans, our house had a separate garage. It was a square, box-like structure and attached to the side nearest the house was a lattice for vines to grow on. I regularly climbed this rather rickety ladder because the roof was covered with tar paper and gravel. On hot days, of which there were plenty, the tar would bubble up into huge globlike bubbles, and anyone who has ever played with such substances can imagine the fun I had on the roof. Come to think of it, my mother would become exasperated with me regularly at the dinner table for playing with the hot wax as it dripped down the sides of the candles. This was almost as much fun as playing with the hot tar. I think this may have been my current expression of pottery in this lifetime.

This may seem absurd as an example, but stop and think about your own life. What are you particularly drawn to that bears some resemblance to a certain activity, or perhaps is the exact activity itself? Do you love building? Find a hammer and some nails and pound them into a piece of wood. How about being on the water? Maybe a fisherman's life is for you? Nursing? Volunteer work at a hospital? Sewing? Try making a dress, a pull-over shirt for yourself or your partner. What about cooking? Have you always wanted to read about philosophy, about painting? Wouldn't it be fun for you to decide to be bold, to strike out and do what you have always wanted to do and not to care if everyone will say you're crazy? I hope some of you will do just this. Even if you feel tied down by life so firmly that you "know" there is no time or money for this radical change, maybe that isn't entirely true, maybe it's because you have never thought you could do it. But, maybe you can!

CHIEF WHITE EAGLE: When you were there as a potter, you were in the body of a woman.

You had small children but the one that was your mate could not stay with you on the earth plane long for he was a man of much bravery and acted as a scout for the safety of all. He was left with an arrow through his heart. You were not alone for there were others who cared for you and for your children. There was a unity within the tribe that made for a giving of love and care to all within their own culture.

You should know that when you walk you are often accompanied by those who were of the Indian realm. They will not always be with you, but there will be times, particularly when you are in the woods or the desert, you will feel their presence.

This is true. I often am aware of spirit presences around me and the feeling of being guided, as well as guarded, is often with me. Prior to my work with Verna, I felt certain that I'd been an Indian in a previous lifetime, or perhaps in several of them. And I've dreamed so often of what this continent must have looked like when there were only Indians here, before we came along to tell them that what they were doing was all wrong and that the things they believed in were also wrong. How beautiful it must have been then.

CHIEF WHITE EAGLE: You had another such existence among my people as an explorer. You were upon an expedition which set out to do a mapping of your country. You walked great distances, and experienced much that made you trust yourself.

You had knowledges then of the use of the berries and other wild foods. You will have these knowledges again. You were sometimes very fatigued and often had the feeling that you could not walk but one more step. The experience I tell you about has carried forward to this lifetime in your knees.

Chief White Eagle's remark was of immediate interest to me, having had troubles involving my knees for several years. Of course the fall I had in Greece two or three years ago didn't help my knees either but that was by no means the beginning of my knee problems. On that day I had climbed the steep stairs clinging to the outside of the small stone house on the island of Aegina, where the great Greek writer Nikos Kazantzakis had lived and worked for many years. From the roof we could see miles of blue water dotted with mountainous little islands, the exquisite Aegean Sea.

Perhaps I was drunk with the beauty around me, but whatever the reason, I was climbing down, with no handrail to hang on to, when I suddenly decided to lean down to pick up one of several cats waiting for us at the bottom of the steps. This was my mistake. I lost my balance, ending up running as one does, across the stone patio, trying vainly to regain my feet. Down I went on to my already vulnerable knees. Such occurrences always make me wonder if my knees are bad because of former life experiences, or do I favor the idea of falling on them to justify the fact that as one born under the sign of Capricorn, I am "supposed" to have bad knees? Maybe both!

CHIEF WHITE EAGLE: The importance of walking silently, so as not to disturb any of the creatures, nor even the plants, is very poorly understood at this time. For the plants feel the disturbance of sound, particularly those sounds that are not in their harmony. The little machines that roar over the land greatly disturb the frequencies of the trees, for the trees, like humans, must compensate for this noise within their own consciousness. I will stop for a moment to see if there is anything that you wish to ask.

KIT: Thank you, Chief White Eagle. The place you speak of, with the sunken lake where the pottery is buried between the City of Angels, and Arizona, would it be before we cross the river to go into Arizona?

CHIEF WHITE EAGLE: I cannot say exactly. I do not know those boundaries, but it is near the little city that you call Blythe.

KIT: Chief, when I'm in Arizona, going to visit the Hopi, I always feel that I'm going home. I believe that I am going to end my days in either Arizona or New Mexico.

CHIEF WHITE EAGLE: You have at other times ended your days there. It will be your own free choice as to where you end your days. But you are not coming to the end of your days for a long time. It is your choice and you have already made this choice. You are aware that you have not yet completed all.

Some years ago when I was living on the northern California coast, I had come down to Santa Barbara for a visit and one night while dining with two friends, I remarked that I was so homesick for the desert that I was thinking of driving down to Arizona alone just to be there again.

One of the friends proposed that she come along, to which I agreed with pleasure. We rendezvoused in the airport in Los Angeles some time later and flew over to Albuquerque from where we set out on our journey. This took us through much of northern Arizona and New Mexico where most of the Indian ruins are situated. We stopped at numerous trading posts, galleries, museums and so on, and from time to time I would buy a pot, a basket, or perhaps a rug. Old ones, always, as I prefer the softness of faded colors.

I remember feeling a certain sense of liberation simply by being back on the land I loved. It was then that I began buying pottery. Occasionally, I pick up some pieces by contemporary potters, those whose work I particularly enjoy. By now my collection, though small, is quite choice, and I have some beautiful baskets as well.

On my trips to the Southwest, the ultimate destination determines where we cross the Colorado River into Arizona and now, every time we cross near Blythe, if I am flying, I look down and clearly see the dry lake bed and wonder. . .

Five months later Indira told me of another Native American lifetime as a woman, again involved with pottery, and her thoughts reflected what Chief White Eagle had said earlier:

INDIRA: We wish to tell you of a lifetime as an Indian woman in your own California state. This was not in your current environment but in the eastern portion of your state. There was flatness, and in the distance could be seen hills.

Indira's words bring to my mind an instant view of the desert along the Colorado River. One of the desert's most appealing aspects for me is just that scenery, that flatness, which she describes, and always with the mountains in the background.

You were in a lady's body and you created potteries, vessels which were used in an everyday basis, work which you enjoyed greatly. It was understood how to heat them and there were ovens that were created in the sand. There was great heat there at different times of the day and this created a reflection which was utilized in the actual baking of the clay. Some were tall shapes that were used as water vessels, others broad-based shapes that were used both to store food as well as basins to eat from.

There were even some that were ceremonial or decorative. But for the most part you were creating things that were very functional, that were very much used. These potteries are still buried here. You would recognize them if you saw them. You would recognize their colors, and perhaps the feel and the vibration of them. There was a lot of pink, some grey, and they were made of clay from a riverbed which was there at that particular time.

KIT: A few weeks ago, Chief White Eagle told me almost exactly what you're telling me, Indira, about the western part of Arizona.

INDIRA: It would be most fascinating to look there, for some will tell you that there was no culture there, you understand? But of course, there was.

Note that Chief White Eagle spoke of Western Arizona, while Indira described it as the eastern part of California. Both identified pink and gray as the predominant colors in the area and it seems that both areas are only separated from each other by the Colorado River.

Indira went on to tell me of a mate I had at that time. This was a lovable man, at least he was in my eyes, although in our tribe he was not thought of highly. The culture was one in which everyone worked, and for him not to do so lost him the respect of the others. Watching me work on the pottery seemed to mesmerize him and he was content to sit in the sun and do this all day.

This mate reminds me of several other men who have been in my life. Charming, and most definitely not highly-motivated to work. She says that because of this man, I now tend to enjoy being with men who have accomplished things, and this is true.

INDIRA: In another Hopi lifetime, we see you as a woman sitting on the ground, upon a small covering with magnificent designs. This was primarily in brown with white backgrounds. You are holding forth a bit around a bowl. You were more or less starting to become as an elder, people would come to listen to you, to talk with you, and to sit around while you were working on the bowls. There was much learning that occurred here, even though it appeared only that food was being prepared.

Other ladies would gather around to listen, because they knew there was much wisdom that had been garnered through your experience. You had lost a mate and there was much closeness that had been there, so you experienced a serious grief by this loss. There was a ceremony for expressing grief, and there were several ways in which this was done. But after this expression of grief, it was as though you detached yourself from it. You had the knowledge within your heart. You would not have been able to verbalize it really, but you knew within your heart that it had been necessary for him to go into the land of the Great Spirit. And you didn't dwell upon your loss.

There were many who came to talk, and they would rock their babies, and listen, because frequently they were concerned for their own mates who would be on a mission and they never knew who would return or who wouldn't.

You also spoke often on the importance of the sun, and you taught them the importance of the moon. You spoke of the fineness that comes from the land of the Great Spirit. You tried to share and to teach these wisdoms to individuals.

You had that lifetime for several reasons, one of which was to learn to give much love. There was so much love that was given to the mate, even though there was grief, too, when the departure came.

There was understanding that was given to all. There were gatherings, which began with long periods of silence before it was deemed correct to begin with a sacred discussion. There were certain stories that were told over and over about the Great Spirit, and about the planet and about the earth, and about the spirits in the trees, and those on the ground. And all would listen, and it would take days of ceremony to complete this. But when it was done, there was cause for celebration.

According to Indira, I had a very hard lifetime in Russia where I incarnated in the body of a woman who worked with her hands, helping her mate to carry rocks for those who were busy with the building of various structures. We carried them by hand, and Indira says that existence was very similar to life in prison.

There was so little in our lives that at night we had only bowls of watery grain, which we shared with whoever appeared. There was a bed, where we sat to eat, to talk, and at last to sleep. My mate was without hope and one of my karmic tasks was to give him encouragement to help him get through the days and nights. It was a life of dark and gloomy days, years fighting off the despair, and though it was a hard existence, we had each other to help us get through. I am told that this life was given me to learn patience:

INDIRA: You are being shown this difficult and struggling lifetime for a particular reason. It was because you had really no choice, it was circumstance. You had the choice of coming into the round, but once you were born into a body, you had little choice, you could either die or go through the motions. You were building for those that had much of the monetary at that particular time. And you gained through the suffering, and the gentleman did also. Do you understand?

KIT: Yes, he must have. It sounds like a really rough round. It is an interesting life for me to speculate on, however.

INDIRA: It was just as a balancing life really for you, an opportunity to grow in that particular manner, an opportunity to encourage someone totally at close range. You will again be encouraging many many individuals in this particular lifetime, and you will find it easier for you to encourage those who come before you. But the principles are the same.

Through the past years, it is true that I have become aware that I have a gift for the encouragement of others. Sometime a friend has remarked that just hearing my voice on the telephone has given them a lift. I am aware of this and use it often. When I give encouragement in this manner, I consider it of more value than writing a check, which is another method of encouraging another. Although I do that kind of encouraging constantly through my foundation, it always seems to me that, assuming that one has it to give, it is easier to give money, while the giving of oneself is often much more difficult.

KIT: I am very aware of my own changes, my own growth in this lifetime. Losing John brought tremendous growth for me. Once, I heard a voice when I was standing on the sidewalk in Gallup. I was waiting for my friends who were still inside of the restaurant paying the bill and joking with the cashier, when I heard a clear, inner voice—I was told that I was having to go through this bad time for the greater good of the whole. This was a jolting experience for me and the words I heard have proven to be true. That it was John speaking I never doubted any more than I had doubted the evidence of my eyes when I had seen him standing with his hands in his pockets leaning against the wall of the Safeway store in Winslow, Arizona. I began then to realize the changes that were already occurring. Not to me alone, but to his friends and colleagues, too.

INDIRA: It is correct to be honest, self-evaluative, you see, because from this sometimes grows what else you can still do.

But there are those that are afraid because they do not want to do the judgment. Well, they are the only ones ultimately really that are going to judge, you see, whether or not they did a good job. Even God leaves you alone, leaves you to make the judgment.

KIT: How so?

INDIRA: God gives you the free will. And you're always going to be your own harshest judge. It can be positive or negative, depending on how the energy is utilized, once this evaluation has taken place.

KIT: You really do pour information into me fast, Indira. It's hard to keep up with you at times.

INDIRA: We wish to give you a lot upon which to have your own inner assessment. For also, part of what is occurring in these little interactions is that you are being given the opportunity to raise your vibratory sense as a result of these connections.

Not long ago, as I was talking with a friend who owns a bookstore, my glance fell on a somewhat worn-looking book resting on top of the pile of books where we stood talking. The book was about Egypt, and I picked it up, flipped over a few pages while remarking that I had been recently told by spirit to study hieroglyphs and perhaps I should buy this book. My friend looked at it, then said she'd never seen it before. I suggested it might have come from her used book department, and she handed it to me, saying, "Take it, it's yours."

I have not really studied it yet, just leafed through it, and when quite recently another book on Egypt came into my possession, I found the hieroglyphs shown on the front and back most intriguing. What do they mean and why has it come to me? I guess we've all had similar experiences of this kind of karmic synchronicities.

Although I have never felt strongly drawn to the Arab nations, in addition to the life I described earlier with a mate in Egypt who was a builder, I also had a lifetime in Egypt as the wife of a powerful man, according to Indira, a man who was a good steward to all who in any way depended on him, and this bore directly on my love for the land. I was a helpmate to him in the sense that we counseled together regarding all decisions affecting the people, the land, the life of the entire area over which he had stewardship. I learned of this particular lifetime when on one occasion I asked Indira to tell me about lifetimes involving money and material wealth:

KIT: Indira, I'd like you to tell me, if it's appropriate, about a past lifetime of mine in which money played an important part. Because of my relationship with money in this lifetime, I'm curious about the past.

INDIRA: Well, I'm going to tell you a whole stream of things, actually, because it's not just one. You see, this has been coming about for you over the centuries really.

You had a lifetime in ancient Egypt during the time of Ramses I. In this particular time you were consort-mate of one who was in the ruling position. There were many that had positions of money at this time, also power, so to speak. It was not universal of course. There are and always will be, those who serve and those that have the power and those that have the money. But there were inordinate numbers of people who had goods of the world. Do you understand?

KIT: Yes.

INDIRA: But you had monumental goods. Your mate was not the top ruler, but one of those who ruled through teaching. You stood closely by his side.

There were certain days in which individuals could come for assistance. They came for advice, they came for having disputes settled, things of this nature. They came for wide streams of assistance. Now, they were really coming to ask your mate. But you were in such close understanding each with the other, that you would listen silently, and there were times when he would look at you and you would tell him only a word or two, but it was always absolutely correct.

It was because you were seeing into their hearts. You were able to see knowingly and understandingly what was deepest in the heart. You were most generous with what individuals were given at that particular time. Some did not even ask for certain things that were in their hearts. But it was given. At times, it was arranged silently. It was not known even from whence it had come, as though there was a windfall. But there was an understanding which began to develop from those who had come to see this particular ruler. They were soon experiencing profoundly of good fortune, each in his or her own way.

And it was frequently because you nodded, or you gave the extra suggestion to the mate. And it so enriched their lives, that there was, how shall I say it correctly, it was as though you were making a *spiritual stockpile* for yourself. It wasn't that you were consciously going to receive anything back from any of these individuals.

To some was given land. It was an unheard of benefit at that particular time, for those that had not acquired it through the father. And the profoundness of their sudden fortune, to have their own plot of land, was very overwhelming to them. Do you understand?

KIT: It must have been wonderful.

INDIRA: And so it was. To some there was given oxen that lightened their load. To some there was given profound wisdom, understanding that they took with them all their lives. So there was much, much giving. There was not so much giving to this mate at this particular time, nor he to you, but there was much spontaneous giving. It wasn't that you were relying on him, for once you became his consort, you were as it is said in your world today, 'set for life.' There wasn't anything you needed, you see? Everything was provided for.

KIT: In spiritual ways as well?

INDIRA: Indeed, in spiritual understanding you had training beyond all in the land. And so did your mate. There were other rulers who abused their privileges, but you and your mate used them wisely. As you gave, you still had more than sufficient always. Do you understand this principle?

KIT: Of course, and it still works.

INDIRA: As the principle was not distorted, much was given to the universe. And as you gave it was simply put there for your own future use. You are drawing upon it at this particular time.

In this lifetime you also chose to instruct. There would come to you habitually, the women, those that were of the serving class. They would bring their children with them. Although it was correct for these women to go into the temples to pray, it was not generally done that they would be given instruction in simple matters of life. They were given instructions on how to take care of their bodies, how to care for their children, even, when it was time for them to desire no more children, how it was done. They would use simple pebbles, special ones in which there were certain emissions. These were gotten from certain portions of Egyptian land that would emit certain vibrations. It served as what you term your birth control purpose.

These ladies would be summoned by those that were serving you, and you would sit with them and encourage them to express themselves. They asked many questions relating to their children and to their general welfare. You offered also instructions in matters of the spirit. It was as if you were building a foundation for the present during that particular lifetime.

I wonder how many times I have looked with envy on two people serving as these two did, both involved in life service, both holding the same ideals, the same goals. It always seems to me to be a truly satisfactory way of life. It was what I had for those few weeks with John before he drowned. For both of us the realization was clear that what we were put here to do during this lifetime was to serve others.

I have learned that growth comes about with rough times, hard lessons to learn, hard passages to work through, rarely if ever through pleasant lifetimes devoid of conflict. My two marriages gave me plenty of strife with many things to work on. For most of us it seems, our share of hard blows is inevitable and I long ago recognized it to be one of the facts we must cope with. What helps us grow is how we handle these rough spots.

I was so overwhelmed with grief after I lost John that I didn't know how I would ever put my life together again. But I did, and it wasn't many months before I knew that his death was as important for me as our brief time together had been. I doubt though, that I could have accomplished my recovery without loyal and loving friends and for them I am ever grateful.

When my daughter died in the summer of 1985, I knew that again it would be a learning experience for me. It is a terribly hard blow to lose a child, and in the natural course of life it is out of context somehow. I miss her terribly and find myself often thinking I'll call her and tell her something amusing or interesting, only to realize with a shock that I can no longer do that. But in spite of the pain, the fact is that we all, her brother and her sister, as well as myself, are growing as a result of our loss.

According to what Indira told me, John and I had shared only one other lifetime, on the island of Lesbos in Greece.

INDIRA: This man, John, had great growth experiences and philosophical learnings in that part of the world (Greece), as did you yourself. It was during the period in which there was still what you call the Libraries of Alexandria, and you probed, you studied and searched, and spent a lot of time on what would be called historical information.

KIT: How was it that we had access to the library of Alexandria?

INDIRA: Because you were privileged, royalty is not the right word. Privileged is a better word. And so you and this man were together in that time, doing that work.

KIT: Since John left his body, I have found out repeatedly about things which we were both involved with but we had never met at any of those places or events.

INDIRA: Let me put it this way, the vibrations were always there, whether you were in the particular sites or not.

On another occasion, I asked Indira about John Tomson in spirit, and what was happening to him on that plane:

INDIRA: What is occurring with this gentleman is this— there is a lot of what you call decision-making. When we say this, he is deciding upon three possibilities of more intensive study upon other spheres. One, it is as though there is a study of symbols that is becoming important to him. He had some innate awareness of this. This gentleman could have looked at rocks, at carvings, at whatever was preserved, and if he had spent— he did not spend a lot of time upon this—but if he had spent some time upon it on the earth plane, he would have been able to take into his hands certain symbols and known what they meant, but he is now contemplating that as one avenue of study. The second thing is that he is contemplating what we would call the study of certain types of musical forces. This is being done because of the importance that this will have upon the earth plane and it is felt that if he goes upon this study, that he can be of assistance to others upon the earth plane in transmitting this. He would be most amenable to transmitting it to you and to others close to you if you so desire this, as he goes upon more relearning himself.

It is also thirdly that he is contemplating going upon the study of the various effects that waters have upon the human body, since a large part of the body is made up of water as an element. This may seem a strange study, but it is of very great importance. All cultures have used water in some way or another— water as principle of purification, of rebirthing, of the flow of life, as a principle of what you call knowing. At the moment, actually, the water holds out. It is a bit strange and he laughs a little out loud at this particular irony for some reason. I don't understand it. But at any rate, this is one of the things that he has high upon the mind.

KIT: You know, Indira, during this round I have left two husbands, neither of them wanting me to go. I've thought about this a lot. Of course, the fact that I am independently wealthy helped make it possible. But I have wondered if perhaps my finding John, falling in love with him, only to have him taken from me in so short a time, I have wondered if this might have been sent me as a balancing out, so to speak?

INDIRA: How do you mean, a balancing of what?

KIT: A balancing for my having left and hurt those two men, to have the one I really loved taken from me.

INDIRA: No, it was not in this regard. You had an opportunity to learn much from these gentlemen, and that is why they were sent to you. And they learned from you as well.

KIT: It is true, of course, that I learned much from all of them and I began knowing some months after John's death that the very fact of his having lived, done the things he did, been the catalyst that he was, just as I am myself, was of tremendous importance. Many circumstances began to alter markedly for many people. All kinds of things started happening, things which would never have occurred if John hadn't died.

I learned a tremendous amount about his life experiences on this plane, not from John alone, but from his friends and family, as we knew one another such a short time. It was a time of great growth for me, and in fact, has never ceased being just that.

John's interests in this life closely paralleled mine. He had
established, with several other men and women, a foundation which
undertook a number of different projects. Much of this work revolved
around Native Americans and he had many friends among them
suggesting to me that he, too, had experienced lifetimes as an Indian.
He was, as I have said elsewhere, living on the Hopi reserve when we
met, just beginning to work on a project for the Hopi. Now that I think
of it, he may have been the mate whose loss I grieved for in one of my
Hopi lives.

KIT: You told me a few weeks ago, Indira, that if John were
living I would not be on the search that illuminates my life now.
And I replied that I am very aware of this. How strange and
wonderful that the greatest sorrow of my life brought me the
greatest growth and learning. Three years ago, this would have
been literally impossible for me to believe.

INDIRA: You were given a lot, although on the earth plane
it was very harsh for you. But for your higher aspects, it was
monumental. Do you understand this?

KIT: I do understand and recognize the importance of this.

INDIRA: So, it was an opportunity for a lot of learning and
also an opportunity for a lot of love. From this, as a matter of
fact, you learned as much as you did from your two mates.

KIT: More. I learned a lot and still am.

INDIRA: Well, however you evaluate it, but this was not by
accident, and it was not as a balancing. There is not to be felt any
onus, any of what you term guilt from your leaving those two
mates, for this was in the correctness.

KIT: Well, if I think of it in terms of my self, which is how I
have to do, it was in the correctness indeed.

INDIRA: You see, it's often misunderstood. It is, of course,
correct and necessary to take others into consideration, but
ultimately, it's your own soul that has to be given first crack, so
to speak. It is not always done on the earth plane and it causes
havoc. You see, if there were more attention paid in this
particular regard and in this particular aspect, it would be very
beneficial for all. There will be those that will cry selfishness,
you see, but that is only meant to keep others under control.

KIT: How do you mean that?

INDIRA: There will be those who will say it is selfish of you to leave, you see. Or it's selfish of you to do this or that. Well, on the surface it may even appear at times to be selfish. But it is your own soul growth that you must always attend to for the largest and to the highest always.

KIT: Okay, I understand what you're saying. It really has to be that way.

INDIRA: That is correct. There isn't any choice. It is not that you must create hardships for others. That is not permissible. But only so that really, ultimately it is your own soul and your connection with God that is of the highest importance. And it is quite truthful really, if you look at these two gentlemen that you supposedly left, that you did what you could, actually, in order to lead them and to elevate. And then it was time to leave, you see.

KIT: That's true, I feel sure, in many relationships, isn't it?

INDIRA: Well, it can be. There are some relationships that are made to continue. Others are not meant to.

KIT: Of course.

INDIRA: It is as a fine line sometimes, as to when it is appropriate to leave. But that too, can be decided.

Fittingly, a friend planted an olive tree on a hillside on the island of Lesbos, in John's memory. I enjoy thinking of that little grey-green tree on that hillside letting the breezes blow through its leaves, and the hot Greek sun shine down upon it.

Some day I will go to visit that tree.

CHAPTER SIX

The Essenes, President Reagan, and John Lennon

DURING MY FIRST TWO YEARS of working with Indira, I had a few sessions with Kevin Ryerson, the San Francisco-based medium whose work with Shirley MacLaine was chronicled in her book, *Out on A Limb*.

As a friend of Verna's Spiritual Sciences Institute, Kevin periodically gives public and private readings in Santa Barbara, and I found him to be a charming man, as well as a practiced channel.

In appearance Kevin presents a romantic, rather dramatic figure. It would be appropriate for him to wear a cape and a broad-brimmed soft hat, over a ruffled shirt and a bottle-green velveteen jacket. I see I am describing the way another romantic looking man, a friend now long dead, used to dress, but it would suit Kevin Ryerson as well.

In her book, MacLaine described her first meeting with Kevin, saying that he'd come dressed all in beige, a bit on the theatrical side, or, as she put it, "straight from Western Costume." Shirley went on to make an important point about people's appearances, and the way we often form our initial snap judgments from these first impressions—but having had experiences with trance channels, I was already aware that mediums, like people in general, come in all shapes, sizes and colors.

At both of my sessions, Kevin's spirit guide, John, who lived during the time of Christ, came through, as well as Tom Macpherson, the spirit of a humorous Scotsman who described himself as having worked for the British government as a diplomatic spy in the 1600s. As such, he was familiar with the psychological as well as psychic forces which interact in the world we know as politics.

Here are his opening words to me:

TOM: I'd like to pass on to you a brief example of what I do believe some of your work is all about. For instance, would you say you have been somewhat of a politically active creature over the years?

KIT: Ummm, yes, for the better part of my life I have.

I want to emphasize here that at the time, Kevin Ryerson had never heard of me, nor of the extent of my involvement with politics. I consider it a state of grace that I was born with a social conscience and have all of my life been driven by it to act in whatever ways I can in support of the oppressed, the underdog.

TOM: Well, then I would like to give you an example of the equivalent of our New Age thought and the way it has impact on the political and social events on the earth plane. Would you be intrigued with that?

KIT: Most definitely.

TOM: Well, are you familiar with the so-called twenty-year cycle? Where every twenty years or so, your president who is elected in a zero year dies in office? Well, your Reagan fellow was the last president elected in a zero year, do you understand this?

KIT: Yes, 1980.

TOM: I do believe that when your Mr. Kennedy was shot in office—having been elected in 1960—there was a *positive* side to the horrible event, a catalytic effect. It motivated people to put much of his civil rights legislation in order, and it motivated many people on an emotional and political basis to cause sweeping social change. Is this fairly correct?

KIT: Yes, it is my opinion that is what happened. It seems to me this concept would also apply to Abraham Lincoln. He was elected in 1860, and he also died in office. Lincoln's intentions for a united North and South became a reality only after his assassination.

TOM: Very well. Now, to a certain degree, what was transpiring in this last cycle is that with the economy as low as it was, when Mr. Reagan was shot there was the rather nasty potential of having exactly the opposite happening—that is, *negative* social effects.

It might have had reverberations similar to the period of your Joseph McCarthy era, the conditions of that time. Because, had your Mr. Reagan died, there would have been an extreme, right-wing backlash.

But what offset that, if you will, happened just six months before. Do you remember when the English balladeer, Mr. John Lennon was shot?

KIT: Yes.

TOM: Well, millions of people were getting ready to mourn for him, and I do believe the widow, Yoko Ono, said: "Do not pray for John, pray for the planet." And there were millions of lives linked across the planet in a single moment praying for its well-being. And it was because of this outpouring of positive consciousness directed toward the planet that six months later, when your Reagan man was shot, there was not the backlash and negativity which might have been released. Isn't it a fascinating concept?

KIT: Yes it is, Tom, and it reminds me in a way of something that's happened in my life.

Almost three years ago I met and fell very much in love with a man and he with me and we began living together. He had been married three times, and I twice. And he had had lovers as I had had lovers, but when we met we both felt as if we'd finally come home.

A few weeks later, though, he drowned. We had such a short time together, but not long after his death, he manifested himself to me leaning against the wall of the Safeway store in Winslow, Arizona, of all the bizarre places for a mystical experience.

I was staying with my Hopi friends on the reservation, in the house where I had first met John, and my hostess Fermina

Banyacya and I had gone to Winslow for the weekly Safeway run. There was a heavy snowstorm outside, and as Fermina was still in the store wheeling her heavy basket around, I told her I would bring the car up to the door so she wouldn't have to plow across the driveway in the snow.

I was sitting in my car listening to music and waiting for her to come out when all of a sudden I saw John standing there. Everyone was inside and there, on that big empty covered porch-entrance stood John, dressed in a dark blue windbreaker, light khaki pants and a white shirt. He was simply leaning against the wall, looking thoughtfully at me. I remember thinking he was dressed lightly for such a cold day as the blizzard was quite severe by this time.

Needless to say, I was astonished. I looked away, as a sort of test, I think, and each time I looked back, he was there. His hands were in his pockets, and he simply stood there being visible to me for a small period of time. And then, finally, he was no longer there. I have been told by spirit that it takes an enormous amount of energy for one already in the spirit to manifest in that way. Two of his long time friends also saw him after he had made the transition.

Some time after this, but still not long after his death, I was driving from the Hopi reservation up to Albuquerque. There were four of us, my three companions, a Navajo, a Hopi and the other an Anglo, all friends and colleagues of John's for many years. We had stopped in Gallup, New Mexico, for lunch, and as the three men were standing talking and laughing with the cashier, I decided to wait outside in the sunshine for them.

It was cold and windy and as I stood on the sidewalk watching the shadow of my hair blowing around, a voice spoke inside of my head. The voice said to me that I was having to go through this bad time for the greater good of the whole and that's exactly what happened. And I feel like that's what you're telling me about John Lennon, that he died for the greater good of the whole.

I thought I would never recover from the grief, but I did, and it strengthened me in my commitment to serve others. I know this awareness of working for the greater good of the whole, is responsible for my ever-increasing involvement in world affairs as well as spiritual matters.

I ran into a friend just yesterday whose first question was what I thought about the recent local elections. She was surprised at my lack of concern, although the outcome of our elections certainly hadn't pleased me. But it is clear to me now that when you begin thinking in cosmic terms, your whole viewpoint is irrevocably altered. This is not to say that your concern for the individual, for your fellow human and humanity as a whole, is diminished; quite the contrary, in fact. It's just that you approach it from a radically different perspective.

KIT: Tom, it seems to me that everything will be balanced out eventually. And my experience with John's spirit is similar to the kind of manifestation you're talking about after John Lennon's death. Rather than praying for the man, be aware of the needs of the planet and work towards that end.

TOM: That would be correct.

KIT: I have a question about karma. I've been working with the homeless a lot in the last year and a half, and with others who are in trouble, in pain, with problems of one sort or another. But I'm trying to understand the nature of giving help to people—when we can help, when to pull back and so forth.

TOM: I think I understand what you're asking, and it is a tricky issue. I would have to say that it is keeping of the old commandment of loving God, and your neighbor, as yourself.

This reflects Indira Latari's injunction to me regarding the two most important lessons we come to learn, namely: to know and love ourselves and to know and to love God. And strange though it may appear, we cannot do the second until we understand the first. If we accept the concept, no, the awareness, of ourselves each being a part of God, we more clearly understand that until we know the smaller part of God, namely each one of us, we will not know the larger.

When we are first introduced to the concept of loving ourselves, I imagine that most of us find all too many qualities in ourselves that we have never come to terms with. But all I can say is, keep trying, people, it is worth it.

TOM:It is to make peace with every individual, and also to aid where possible. For instance, if you extend a helping hand and it is rejected, then the most at that time that can be done is to stand with the hand open, extended. But not to let yourself get pulled into the water. Otherwise, you just have two people who are sinking, versus at least one that is waiting on the shore in a position to help.

Sometimes you have to go a bit farther and throw the person a lifeline. But you must stand on your own firm ground, as they say. The real key is that as you continue to progress on your own way of transformation, those people will be able to take inspiration from you, because of the common bonds that are there between the two of you.

An example of this could be seen in the story you just related, when your friend drowned. If you had stopped in your progress and become bogged down in the emotionalism of the issue, of the trauma, then your life might have begun to fold in upon itself. You might not have been able to recoup from it and to put it into its appropriate perspective. Then, possibly, you would have been in a position similar to those who become crippled, and we do not mean just physically. The way some of those whom you would now like to aid have become.

Finally, the way really to aid others is by continuing on with your own progress. By progressing *yourself* you then can make the statement by which others might be able to light the spark of their own inspiration, to recoil or rebound from whatever their negative circumstances might be.

This has proven to be true with me. I have, for some time now, been increasing my concentration on my own spiritual growth, and somewhat to my own astonishment, I find others seeking me out for advice, for counsel, for whatever it is that I have to give. Needless to say, I am grateful to be able to assist or serve, in whatever manner is most helpful.

KIT: That makes a lot of sense to me, Tom. I have no real complaints now, about my life. I sometimes think I would like to have another companion, but then I think I'm not so sure that's the right thing for me to do now. It's very peaceful living by myself.

TOM: I do believe this would be an area pretty much of exercise of your free will. Because let me give you a hint. I believe that you are no longer working on karma on the earth

plane, so much as you are working more on dharma, your service. Do you understand this?
KIT: Yes, I do.
Although I agreed that I understood Tom's comments, on reflection I came up with a different meaning. I believe that Tom meant that I had spent the first part of my life working on my karma, getting myself ready, I suppose, for my present life, which concerns itself very much with dharma, i.e. service to my fellow humans.

Now, I wonder how many of my readers have experienced similar life patterns? It occurs to me that perhaps most of us spend the early part of our lives in a kind of preparation, resolving certain basic karmic conditions, whether family-oriented or relationship-oriented, so that we can then go on to the dharma—or service aspects—of the latter part of our lives.

Approaching the end of this round as I am, and anticipating the evaluation period I believe we undergo after our spirits leave our bodies, I see many opportunities that I had, opportunities for growth, for the expression of love and compassion, which I lost or did not respond to. Indira has told me that this review period immediately after death of the physical body "can be painful for persons," and with knowledge I have now, I can easily see why.

I was talking just now with my editor and friend Steve Diamond, about the advent of New Age children, how many were being born when his generation came along, the so-called Baby Boomers, and how many more are constantly coming into bodies on this planet as we lurch toward the Millenium, and I was reminded of a friend of my first husband, years ago in New Orleans. This man was a theosophist and wielded considerable influence on Ted, as I recall. I remember Ted telling me that this friend had a theory about the many children who were being born in California and who were demonstrating remarkable qualities, showing signs of very advanced beings. I found this man totally out of my realm, but what I was too young and ignorant to see was that had I been more perceptive, and receptive, I could have learned from him. As is so often the case when we are young, my values at the time needed considerable readjusting.

I am guessing that many of you who now find yourselves world servers can look back and remember early days of working on your karma, as of course we are all still doing, only the emphasis has changed toward the dharma side, world service, so to speak.

John, the spirit-teacher also channeled by Kevin Ryerson, is a very different spirit entity than Tom MacPherson. John is said to have lived at the time of Christ and is thought to have to been one of the disciples. John speaks in a quiet voice, almost a whisper, in fact, and his terminology is quite Biblical. After the session, I asked Kevin about the John entity.

"John is very skillful in the sense of indirectly skirting certain questions," Ryerson told me, "such as being asked 'Were you one of the disciples?' But John always likes to think of himself as an individual who studied with Jesus per se, rather than making a big deal out of being one of the twelve disciples."

Unlike Indira, who begins to give me information as soon as she comes in through Verna, John almost always starts with a simple, "Hail. Question?"

When I spoke with John, I asked him if he could give me more information about my lifetimes lived among the Essenes, an area which Indira had discussed with me several months earlier. I knew little of the Essenes when I'd first heard from Indira that I'd had a few incarnations amongst those Dead Sea, communalist, "God-intoxicated mystics"—a phrase I'm borrowing from one of my favorite writers Edward Abbey, with suitable apologies and thanks. The Essenes were a Jewish brotherhood which came into existence around the second century before Christ.

Indira had informed me that I had possessed certain knowledges of the arts of hypnotic healing and such, and what I was told by John through Kevin Ryerson fit perfectly with the earlier information channeled through a different medium and from an entirely different spirit:

JOHN: First, there were at least three lifetimes spent amongst the Essenes, dating back to the true foundation of the Essenes in the Order of Melchizedek.

However, the lifetime spent as an Essene which we now address was when ye were carnate at the founding of the temple by Elijah at Mt. Carmel.

Ye were of mixed ancestrage of Hebrew and Greek, and were one of the individuals who studied the methodologies of Essene divination and consultation. From your Greek background you had a desire to organize the bodies of knowledge into the sciences that they were felt to be. This particular prevalence in the organization of the Mystery School was because the schools of prophets at Mt. Carmel were directly the forerunners of the Essenes who would establish their libraries at Qumram and become the nucleus for those who would eventually be expecting the man Jesus. For we find that the word Essene means precisely that, "expecting."

Having had trouble with organizing things all of my life, this information at first surprised me but I believe that my work with Richard Parker on the foundation can perhaps fall under the head of organizing. I have found that in many cases I am a good worker, but need direction in some areas. What I do very well is to be a catalyst. I know people from all over the planet, and opportunities are constantly given me to bring them, or their projects and needs together, and I try to do it as often as I am able.

I find no reason to doubt that many of those I know and work with today are people with whom I have incarnated before, perhaps many times. Verna Yater, for example, is one; my editor Steve Diamond, another; but there are many with whom I work and walk the same path as before, all of us continuing our contributions to growth and learning in our own ways.

JOHN: As an Essene, those who were primarily respected for their vast knowledges of natural laws of the universe, their abilities of prognostication or predicting, their healing arts, and various other forms, ye were one of those who encouraged the distribution of information.

Distributing information and counseling are exactly what I have been and continue to be involved in, not only through the work of my foundation, but through my own efforts as well. Since coming into my own self-awareness, and my desire to work for the greater good, I have supported numerous publications, documentary films, journalists, researchers, writers on political subjects, including those involved with raising the consciousness of people everywhere, and the consciousness of the planet as a whole. I sometimes speculate on all the others who are, like myself, living the life of world servers, and periodically I wonder how many of them are taken with the sense that they have been engaged in similar service endeavors in previous existences.

I feel sure this explains my sense of excitement on first learning of the Mystery Schools. The very name suggests no boundaries for the imagination. Rahotapaman, the Egyptian priest who has spoken to me a few times through Verna's channeling, told me of the initiations I have undergone in past lives. It occurs to me that these ceremonies are most likely linked to the ones during the Essene era.

From what my teachers in the spirit world tell me, this ancient knowledge of the Mystery Schools is again coming into our consciousness. It has been said also that before this century has ended, mankind will again understand the true powers of the crystal, knowledge of dematerialization, re-materialization, and all the other lost mysteries as well. John continued with his information on my lifetime living in the desert east of the Dead Sea:

JOHN: By no means were the Essenes necessarily a homogeneous group without differences of opinion. Some felt that they must totally withdraw from the world. Others felt that their knowledges should be shared.

Ye were as one of those who helped communicate so that the school should establish ties with other schools throughout Persia, Greece, and Egypt. You also established ties through the various trade routes penetrating into the Indus Valley, exchanging with all kinds of bodies of scholars, even with the Brahmans of India.

In those ways, then, we find that ye are now in a position similar to that Essene existence—seeking avenues to explore and to open up new bodies of information, new areas for individuals to explore for knowledge they already contain within themselves.

We would only say that in these days ye are beginning to reconstruct an equivalent of life purpose from the days past, wherein ye are now coming into the fulfillment and the light and the understanding of thy days, and that indeed ye may build networks and bridges between various persons in seeking through thy stimulation into bringing about and manifesting that which ye call the New Age. For the New Age lives in the hearts and in the minds of individuals and there exists the need to have a forum in which to express that new light that dwells within them. Ye be an individual who shall create that forum. Is this to thy understanding?

KIT: Yes, and I'm grateful knowing that I have been able to play a part in the spreading of a New Age consciousness. When we start our discussion group on Saturdays, during the meetings and after, I remind my friends that it's very important that we send out thoughts of love and support particularly to world leaders at this time so that our help will be expressed in a vibrational way. It's only through every person expressing the positive light that the influence is going to be able to come.

Since John was speaking from the time of Christ, what we call the Biblical era, I decided to question him about some information I'd received from a friend concerning the ancient use of the sacred mushroom, *amanita muscaria*. My friend had suggested that many of the references in the Bible to the actions of particular individuals were really attributable to the mushroom and the psychedelic visions they produced:

JOHN: This is incorrect. You will find that when I speak on this, it is with authority. During the early days of the development of the church, there were many individual splinter factions who took up the Christian teachings. Some of the more accurate elements were a mixture of the actual teachings of the Master, or the man Jesus. The Essene workers and certain ascetic groups who used various forms of psychotropic substances, amongst them this plant, adopted and labelled the plant itself as though it were Christ or the messenger.

Ye have recently received similar groups in thy own early 1960s where they said that the substance known as your LSD was also a similar liberator, and ye have seen similar cult groups arise around other particular methods of opening the doors of consciousness. However, ye would find that the Bible itself is a literal text. It is a historical text of the historical figures, with historical writings of the historical acts. True, at times the actions of those individuals are metaphorical or synonymous with activities on the higher planes.

I myself took LSD once fifteen years ago, and although I do not write this as a recommendation for others to do the same, I know that my entire life was altered in those few hours that I was under the influence of the drug. It actually changed my life that afternoon.

I realized for one thing, that what I had been doing all my life was merely intellectualizing, and I realized further that intellectualizing wasn't what life was all about. I suddenly knew that there was only one thing of importance, and that was love. It turned me around completely and I've really tried to live my life along those lines ever since. I was asked once how I manifest this love. I replied that I manifest it in as many ways as I possibly can, from small, seemingly insignificant ways to important big ones. When the question was asked it was at my own table, where I had several guests for dinner. My good friend Michael was visiting me at the time, and the guests were out-of-town friends of his. Michael was sitting next to me, and taking his hand, I replied that for instance when my friend had friends from out of town, I invited him to bring them to dinner with me as an expression of my love. In the cosmic scheme it is minimal, certainly, and yet, every expression of love has its cosmic importance.

JOHN: You would find that we do not condemn entirely the idea of the use of psychotropic and psycho-stimulating substances. However, it is in the capacity of each individual to tread a path of meditation that may prove sufficient stimulation, for this is the more sophisticated and the more truthful path.

KIT: And certainly the more easily available one.

JOHN: Correct.

Six months later, on Feb. 20, 1985, I had my second session with the entity known as John speaking through Kevin Ryerson.

I had recently learned about the passing of Jane Roberts, the woman who had channeled *The Seth Material, Seth Speaks,* and the other books and information which had come through from Seth. I asked John if Seth would return to speak through another channel.

JOHN: Yes, the one known as Seth will return to speak through many. That individual desires not at this time to necessarily raise up another singular instrument to such similar degree of public prominence. He wishes to disburse the energies over many mediums to diversify teachings that they brought into one centralized body of knowledge. Is this to your understanding?"

I said that it was, and then John told me that Seth had already come through several channels since Jane Roberts' death.

KIT: When I spoke with you before, you told me that I had had three Essene lives. I see the desert, when I think about that previous era, but I don't ever quite see the life that I led. I wonder if you could tell me more about it?

JOHN: You were skilled as a scribe in those days, preserving the old traditions. The Essenes were worshippers of nature, and often invoked the angels of the sun, the angels of the four seasons, and were indeed highly similar to the Taoists in their systems of thought.

In fact, the Essenes were such extensive travelers that they traveled thoroughly to the regions of India and penetrated even into Tibet, always searching for the knowledges that others had to share with them and at the same time to give of their own wisdom. They had extreme degrees of influence from the Brahmans, the Taoists, and the Buddhists. Thy attraction to both nature and the desert comes from time spent amongst Essenes. They were a sophisticated group of individuals who worked with the forces of nature, lived an ascetic life in the desert, a life of simplicity though abundance.

The life described here is one I dream of. To live in nature, living in rhythm with the four seasons, working with nature's forces, living with literate and spiritually-inclined people, for myself I could never ask for more.

JOHN: The Essenes were divided into four quarters. There were the extreme ascetics who were central to the community and maintained the libraries and perhaps were some of the deeper masters of the community. The second order of the Essenes would raise families, and the third order could marry and have full sexual expression in the exchange, raise children and live within the full aesthetics of the community, if they so chose. The fourth order were those who were considered the gentile, that is, outsiders, but who were more than welcomed into the community—these included the transitory influences, such as the merchants and those that traveled the trade routes. In actuality, the Essenes were open to all. They were Semitic, but considered themselves a religious order rather than a racial order."

Steve Diamond, my friend and editor, had a session with Verna Yater, the channel, during the course of our work on this book, and when he asked Indira if he, Verna and I had ever incarnated together he was told that we had, and that it was not by chance that we have been brought together in this lifetime, or "round" as it is termed by spirit. I am including some of the information from that session as it reflects directly on information given to me from John on lifetimes amongst the Essenes:

INDIRA: You three, (Verna, Kit, and Steve) weren't brougt together just by chance. You have been together a number of times, once among the Essenes. In that time and place, you were working in concert, but it was as teaching and also the preservation of information. You will again preserve information. It isn't only to be given out, it's also to be preserved. You each had a somewhat different role, but each was a teacher in that era.

The one that is the channel at this particular time (Verna Yater) was a great preservationist of documents, and worked with those that became the Dead Sea Scrolls. She was most insistent that everything be preserved even though there was communication from spirit that it might not be possible to preserve everything. You will find again that there is the need to at times simply preserve and go on a certain segment, you see?

The one that is known as your Kit in the moment was one that understood quite widely the arts in the realm of how to deal with persons, individuals of different natures. She was not always within the particular community, but would travel to the cities, in the spreading of information.

Indira went on to tell Steve that he served as a scribe, putting down the information and teachings on papyrus and making certain that not only was it correctly written for future preservation, but also that those then living were clear in their understanding of the information. Steve has been a writer all of his life in this round which couldn't be more appropriate.

Indira continued telling Steve about the customs of the time. The Essenes worshipped the sun, worshipping it as The Light, meaning God, and daily there were ceremonies welcoming the sun and its effect on our planet.

At such times prayers were said, the ancient musical instrument called the shofar was sounded, and at other times a ritual dance, not unlike what we now know as Tai Chi, was performed.

She goes on to describe several aspects of life amongst the Essenes. Some lived in caves, considerably removed from the others, some were in the cities, others went about, as I did, spreading the light, transmitting the knowledge, only returning to centers such as Qumram for reconnection, so to speak, with the other members of their particular communal camp, as well as their reconnection with nature.

They were knowledgeable about their bodies as well as their minds, and their children were taught self-hypnosis, allowed to explore and become familiar with the dream state. They were also encouraged to interpret the dreams and were assisted in this by their elders.

INDIRA: Included in all this 'curriculum' as you might call it, quite naturally, was the study and knowledge of the stars. Some specialized in it, and went on to more intensive study, but it was generally common knowledge among the group. There was also much preparation of the beauty surrounding them and their dwelling places. Although it is sometimes thought that it was austere, well, only austere in that there wasn't a lot of the extraneous present. But there was magnificent beauty in the form of poetry, and magnificent beauty that was created in the form of tapestries. But all of it was in simplicity—it was not a cluttered existence in any way.

My tastes today are similar. I can't bear clutter, although anyone looking at my desk, or even at times my dining room table, loaded as it often is with papers, papers, and more papers, would see it and think, that woman must be miserable being surrounded by all that mess. And to be truthful, it does make me uncomfortable to tolerate it. Sometimes I stop and wonder when I think I can ever improve it, but I honestly don't know how. Might it be a karmic condition?

At my second session with Kevin Ryerson, John came again and discussed the coming earth changes which have been predicted for centuries and which are now occurring with considerable regularity. I am writing this entry on November 14, 1985, and only this morning I heard on the news about the totally unexpected earthquake and volcanic explosion in Armero, Colombia. A volcano, quiet for five hundred years, exploded yesterday, and the extent of the damage is not yet known, neither the deaths nor the amount of destruction done in the city and the villages which lay just under the volcano's rim, although initial reports have it that more than 25,000 people have perished.

The northeastern coastline of our own country has just been devastated by unprecedented floods, as have the low lying lands in states adjacent to the Gulf Coast. Here in California, earthquakes can always be, if not expected, certainly realized as entirely possible events. With Mt. St. Helens erupting, earthquakes in Europe, floods in Asia, it appears increasingly clear that the ancient predictions are coming true. The planet is warning us that we have abused her too long, and it is high time we listen.

KIT: John, I have some questions about the predicted shift of the earth on its axis which I'm told is going to happen in the next few years—before the turn of the century.

JOHN: First, the shift has already begun. Since the original prophecies by the individual known as Andrew Jackson Davis and the party known as Edgar Cayce, the earth has shifted on its axis a full quarter to a full three-quarters of a degree. The shift that is predicted is only for another four to at most five degrees. This is gradual.

However, in the next ten to fifteen years, the earth will shift by another quarter to almost a full degree. This will cause more radical activities such as continuing volcanic activity in thy North American continent, which is considered extremely peculiar. Also, the reactivation of many volcanos and earthquakes and changes in weather cycles because of same. For instance, the continuing saturation of thy desert lands to the eventual point where they are subtropical.

KIT: That's interesting. Then we need not expect any reversals, we won't expect to go back to what we think of as "normal" weather patterns, because these are going to be normal weather patterns, I suppose. Is this correct?

JOHN: Correct.

KIT: When the quarter shift comes, that will mean major changes, climactically, won't it? And major changes geographically, topographically, with land sinking and land appearing. Will it be like that?

JOHN: It will be gradual. A speeding up of what has been a gradual process to date. For instance, the erosion of lands in southern California, extreme southern, more so towards the Baja in the same area. Erosion by ocean, by tidal forces, so that eventually the area of land will be covered by water.

Those storms and the tremendous tidal forces which were at work and threatened thy own coastline, will be as though gradual. There will be tidal forces similar to those over a process of fifteen to twenty-five years. However, thy own region of Santa Barbara will eventually prove more stable for there is a gradual rising or buckling of the land mass so that the Channel Islands may act eventually as a barrier against these types of forces.

I am heartened, of course, by John's words about the future of Santa Barbara. As it is said to have once been a part of Lemuria, the land mass which disappeared beneath the waters of the Pacific, currently with the similar happening regarding Atlantis, John's remarks about the Channel Islands buckling and rising may refer to the reappearance of Lemuria.

A great deal of what I have been told, about past lives, planetary events, methods of dealing with toxic wastes, etc., has been (or is in processs of being) corroborated by other psychics, whether in books I subsequently have come across, in the daily news, or in trance sessions with other channnels. When this book is published, I will be interested to see how I am labeled. Gullible will surely be one description, mentally unstable may be another—but it really doesn't matter. I am writing what I believe to be the truth and time will tell.

CHAPTER SEVEN

Some Thoughts on
Neutralizing Radiation,
The Earth Shift,
and Native Americans

WE HAVE ALL certainly noticed the devastating environmental changes which have occurred during the past decade or so, to say nothing of the growing threat of nuclear annihilation which has become a realistic as well as psychological factor of human life. In addition to the possibly devastating conditions created by man, there is also the established scientific reality of the earth's shifting on its axis, and with it the potential for cataclysmic planetary changes.

It was at my very first session with Indira that I was made conscious of the imminence of the earth shift, and the possible consequences to be expected as a result. In later sessions, Chief White Eagle would also bring forth information not only on the planetary crisis, but also thoughts on preparations for the momentous changes which lie ahead for mankind during the coming years of transition—including a method of storing seeds for a long-range future during the time of upheaval.

My love for the desert of the Southwest, in addition to the strong inner urge that I have recently been feeling to establish a spiritual retreat or center in that area, continues to draw me back repeatedly. My close friendship with some of the Hopi, whom I visit on their reservation, finds me returning there more and more.

125

When I went to my first session with Verna, September 21, 1983 I'd just returned from a trip to New Mexico. My first question to Indira was about the house I had recently bought in the Albuquerque area, but I also wanted to know if she had any advice for me on several other questions. First about my being there at all. Secondly about the feasibility of living there on a somewhat permanent basis, and thirdly about the coming earth shift, its probable affects, and how best to prepare for it:

INDIRA: One of the reasons that you have been hearing this particular inner voice telling you to move is that you are having the knowledge that there indeed are changes transpiring upon your earth plane. There will be vaster changes coming including changes that will be occurring within the atmosphere itself.

Indira went on to talk about the changes, including the fact that many are already concerned about the earth's shift, environmentalists in particular. It is true that the majority of people are still unaware, but it is clear that this uneasiness over the conditions of our planet is occurring in many places and to many people. Air pollution, acid rain, dying rivers and lakes with many fearing that the oceans themselves will follow, these are all catastrophic events and little is being done to alleviate them.

Indira brought up the melting of a number of ice caps in different parts of the world, and as I write this, bodies are still being dug from the mud and ash caused by the terrible volcanic eruption which happened just days ago in Colombia. This volcano had been extinct for most of four hundred years and the melting of the ice cap on its summit had caused the mud/ash slides, followed by streaming lava as the heat of the volcano was released. I have read that if this volcano follows the pattern of Mount St.Helens a few years ago, a major eruption is still ahead. And the morning news tells of yet another hurricane in the Caribbean threatening both Cuba and the Florida coast, and the Louisiana coast again as well. Another unusual and potentially devastating happening, and they seem to be increasing in frequency.

Indira speaks of the oceans having already risen, an infinitesimal amount at the moment, but due to speed up in the next three to five years. Destruction of the forests worldwide which has been occurring for years releases some of the topsoil and reforestation seems to be happening rarely, and in only small areas. An increasing lack of oxygen all over the planet is directly attributable to the cutting of the trees, as we have been warned by the dolphins.

Barbara Huss, Verna's colleague and co-founder of the Spiritual Sciences Institute, communicates telepathically with dolphins and they warn of disaster unless massive reforestation programs are begun immediately. Recently I had an interesting message myself in a second-hand way from the dolphins.

I had gone for a session with Verna and when I arrived she told me that she and Barbara had just finished a joint channeling where dolphins had communicated again, telepathically as always, through Barbara's channeling. These are not the spirits of dolphins, as is the case when we humans communicate with the spirits of humans now on the other side of the veil. Rather they are the thought-forms of living dolphins directing their messages through her channeling work. After talking for a few minutes, Verna went into trance, and as usual, Indira came through almost immediately.

Indira began with her usual welcoming greeting, assuring me of her pleasure in being with me again, and then told me that the dolphins had still one more message for Barbara and would like me to transmit it to her. The message was as follows:

The dolphins wanted Barbara to be aware that when they and the whales beach themselves, it is not done as a hostile act, but rather to attract man's attention; they are trying to warn us about the frightening effects of the indiscriminate leveling of forests worldwide, as well as man's continued pollution of the oceans.

I can't help but wonder about Humphrey the humpback whale who recently swam up through San Francisco Bay toward Sacramento, the state capital, to the bafflement of naturalists and authorities alike. But now that I think about it, what better place to head for, if you wanted to get media attention, than the state capitol?

The oxygen given off by the trees has been greatly reduced, Indira tells me, which in turn affects the atmosphere, and us, along with it. This is having and will continue to have, increasingly catastrophic effects on the entire planet and all life upon it. Furthermore, it is diminishing the energies available to us.

Indira warns of earthquakes to come, saying they will be less severe in the southwest, also telling me not to fear, rather to look upon all these occurrences as challenges, opportunities for further spiritual, emotional and psychic growth for humanity. She continues with further information regarding the catastrophies liable to occur following the earth's shift on its axis. According to Indira, there will be darkness over the entire planet for a period of seven days. I seem to recall similar references from the pulpit when I was still a churchgoer, references to the darkness which will cover the face of the earth.

Indira paints a picture of earth shift and its aftermath as a period of shortages, of many wounded and dead, the lack of medical supplies, food, water, transportation totally disrupted, a picture of devastation and destruction. Those who survive will again live as our forefathers did in early days, everyone helping everyone else according to their abilities, until the planet has caught its breath, so to speak, and we can once more bring order out of chaos.

Indira again stresses the fact that such sorrows, such hard trials, are sent to us for our own soul growth, these being a part of the life we have chosen. I used to find this truth hard to accept but I have come to recognize it for what it is. If I am still around when this happens, I will have a chance to try out the pioneer life I have always envied. I can't help but wonder how I will cope with it at this late date in my life.

I asked Indira if there is a way in which we, the people here on the planet, can avert this catastrophe and again she tells me that it is a question of working unceasingly to raise our own spiritual consciousness, and to help others to do the same in every way we can:

INDIRA: It is to spiritualize self completely and to help others to open so that they may also spiritualize themselves. This is part of what the entire process is about. The earth's vibration is in preparation for all this. There is a speeding up of vibrations and many don't recognize it, don't know what to do with it although they have a sense of wanting to do something, but not knowing what. . .

My own sense of all this is that I do indeed feel a quickening of pace. That is the only way I can describe my feeling. Maybe this happens to us all as we grow older, but what interests me is that I am calm and content in the knowing that I have all the time I need to finish what I am supposed to do. And at the same time I feel that the planet's vibrations are speeding up rapidly, although I have no evidence of this. I do, however, see increasing evidence of the planetary raising of consciousness everywhere. To my way of seeing it, the increasing interest in spirituality, in psychic phenomena, in spirit communications of the kind I have had through Verna Yater, in growing acceptance of idea of the existence of beings from other planets, these, and other manifestations of our acknowledgement of inner needs, all point to our increasing growth, the increasing expansion of human consciousness.

As I write this I am well aware that many, perhaps most, of my friends, think of me as certainly eccentric, and misguided, if not downright deranged, but it doesn't bother me. I have lived my life following my path with joys and sorrows mixed.

I have survived overpowering grief and lived to look back on it as a chance to learn valuable lessons, one of them being the realization that the grief would never have been possible had not the joy preceded it. I have few regrets and, dear reader, that old saying about not regretting the things we did do but rather regretting the things we did not do. . .believe me, it's true, in my case at any rate. Take risks, accept challenges, only in this way will you progress in your life's journey, not to mention having fun along the way.

INDIRA: The speed-up of planetary vibrations is to meet the challenges which will be forthcoming. You who live upon the planet will also have your vibrations speeded up, those are all part of the same aspects. But the biggest form of preparation will be in the spiritualizing of the self. If this is not done, there isn't any point in doing anything else, really.

There will be opportunities created to take refuge. This may seem slightly erratic since there will be no total refuge, but there will be energy vortexes created on certain points on the earth, in which there will be the opportunity to be together with others who have also raised their vibrations. And there will be directions and further information given at that particular time to those individuals to permit their own appropriate preparation.

There will be the necessity of burying seeds for many years to come. There will be the necessity of being self-sufficient. There will be the necessity, of course, to make preparations for the darkness which will last for approximately a week. All these preparations and more will be needed.

KIT: Now, when I think about the preparations, when I think about the people who are spiritually advanced, I immediately think about the Hopi in Arizona. Their lives are lived according to their spiritual belief, it's a twenty-four-hour-a-day belief, not just "I'll go to church today," or "I'll say my prayers." No, whatever they do is part of their belief. I have had many meals with them in their homes, and have often witnessed the nearly invisible gesture with which a tiny amount of food is removed from a plate as an offering to a spirit. And although I have sometimes cast a surreptitious glance at the table on arising, only once did I ever see the evidence. To this day I'm not sure which being is honored in this way, only that it is of spiritual intent. Also, I think of them as being very pure people in many ways, although like everybody else, they have their human failings. But I think of Hopi as being a place where I would want to be in the event of such a planetary crisis.

My friends are the so-called "traditionals" who have fought so valiantly against the selling of their land to the oil companies and to the mining companies, as has been advocated by the "progressives," often those on the Tribal Councils, and thus pretty much in control of what occurs. It seems as if these people in favor of selling or leasing, have little concern for the land. As one of my friends said to me, "If we sell our land, when the money is gone, what have we left? All we have is our land."

INDIRA: Well, I will tell you that they certainly have carried the promise forward. But there are also many among your own people that are carrying the information forward. It is not to make the distinctions. Well, you can, but it is only to recognize that there are many among your own people, some whom you would not recognize, who have been carrying the information and the promise forward.

There are many things that can be done to help soften the possible impact of this planetary crisis which has already begun. And part of this is to be as kind to the planet as possible. This is not very well understood, but these are closely tied together. The planet itself has been very ill-treated.

And through this there has been much malalignment of what you call the vibrations, much as if you were to mistreat your body all your life. Only the planet has gone on for many, many lifetimes, and has not always been so mistreated. Gradually, however, it has been more and more so. And there are those that are making good inroads to teach others not to so mistreat, while still others pay no attention at all to this problem on your planet.

KIT: That is true, with so many who think only of raping the land for what profit they will gain.

INDIRA: Correct. They are not always listening, and so one of the ways you can get people to listen to this particular aspect of concern is that as they themselves become more actualized, as they themselves become more spiritualized, they can also see all of these things.

That is why we are putting more attention on the aspect of spiritualizing self. Once this is accomplished, you can't help but notice everything around you, whether it be the rocks, or the trees, or the other peoples of the planet.

KIT: It is true for me that lately I seem to be even more in love with what is around me than before, and I have all my life been keenly appreciative of the beauty surrounding me. Just studying the landscape seems almost electrifying at times.

132 THE BUTTERFLY RISES

INDIRA: There are many more coming into spiritual awareness now. Many are upon a search, having an awareness that something is occurring, but they know not what it is. There are many who will actually not understand the technicalities of the change. That's all right, too. It is not the important thing. The important thing is what happens to the spiritualization of their selves.

KIT: As a result of the changes, you mean?

INDIRA: That is correct. That is the only thing that really counts, ultimately. Because everything else is more or less temporal. The body is temporal, the conditions are temporal, and so forth. In your industrialized countries you have altered planetary conditions through all of the refuse which has been created. You will find that there is debris of your nuclear waste which is the most potent force on the earth plane.

KIT: I can believe it.

INDIRA: It can be altered, however, through the use of your energy fields. It can be altered through the vibrational fields. When you identically match the vibrational level of the waste product with a subtle form of vibrational energy, you will successfully neutralize it. This can come about in your existence.

KIT: Please tell me more about this, Indira.

INDIRA: Certain of your nuclear products will have different vibrational levels. They can and will be measured on your earth plane. These, in turn, you can study and create identical vibrational patterns to them which will neutralize when brought together.

KIT: How do you create these vibrational patterns?

INDIRA: Well, that will be up to those upon your earth plane that will understand them correctly. But there are those that do understand it that are called your physicists. They have not thought of matching them and of neutralizing in this particular way. There will have to be much experimentation because it will need to be accomplished under very controlled conditions. Because of the risks, they will want to perform these experiments within chambers, how you call, your cloud chambers.

KIT: Cloud chambers?

INDIRA: Correct. These are known to your physicists. And in this manner can be conducted these experiments upon your wastes. Burying it doesn't do one iota, it contaminates. Containment is only the appearance of a solution, but it is because they don't know what to do with it, your scientists. So they offer containment, trying to pretend it is a solution.

Now, these ultimate solutions will take a bit of doing. It's not so far away, however, and with your present earth technology you can speed them up. There will be some that will look a bit askance upon this information. And say, goodness, you think this will work? But there will be those that can be found that will, at least, have an openness to the potential.

You will be having conversations with some persons with regard to that which you would call 'research' on the subject of your earth plane waste products.

We are speaking of those in particular that seem to baffle persons as to how they can be gotten rid of without total contamination of the earth plane. There are manners of working upon those that will work vibratorily, and it is not to be so naive as to feel that there will be persons that will immediately accept this, but it will be a seed planting among those that will work quietly upon theoretical formations scientifically in the background.

KIT: How will I be able to be of service in this? I really know so little about the subject, though of course I'm concerned about it.

INDIRA: Oh, there won't be any doubt in your mind. There will be persons that will come unto you. You don't have to go seeking them. They will be led across your path, and there will be conversations and such, and you can assist and steer one another.

But there is information that can be utilized in this toxic waste process that will reach the particular vibratory aspects of this waste material. You see, there can be a reduction of toxicity before it is buried, so-called. It will take courage for some to experiment with this, but it will occur. You do not have to feel responsible, but when you are given the opportunity, simply let it mushroom, because the ideas will not be immediately accepted.

Nor will the idea be immediately tested or experimented with either. But there will become some urgency over it that there will be at least some brave souls that will say, "Ah, well, we have nothing to lose, because we don't know how to contend with it anyway. . ."

Of course, there are some ways of contending with it, the primary one being to create less of the toxic waste, but we unfortunately do not see it as a particularly popular solution on your planet.

KIT: Not just now, no. Unfortunately, it's the opposite.

INDIRA: You see, at the moment you don't have the scientific apparatus to completely measure it—but, if you were to take certain aspects of measuring certain portions of rays of the sun, you would find that there are similarities between these solar rays and the vibratory rates of some of your earth plane toxic wastes. If you were able to do this measuring, you could then assess the method to bring about reduction of the toxicities involved. But you can't measure this with the current earth plane equipment.

KIT: Well, so much is going on with ecological information, right now, new things being sought and found.

INDIRA: Well, we give you this information as fair warning so that you'll think to yourself: 'There is the opportunity to steer such and such a person in that direction, or this direction,' and to start the potential catalytic movement going.

KIT: I will try to act as a catalyst in this matter when the opportunity arises.

INDIRA: Yes, just as you serve as a catalyst for those who are closest to you. Because they are still the ones that must do the actuality of the deeper search. They are the ones that must make the forays into their own territory. You can serve as one who mirrors or gives the opportunity to assess the potential.

As long as the scientists and physicists on your earth plane keep looking for answers, they're going to have a difficult time. When they *start asking questions* then suddenly they'll come to new insights. That is what will assist them immensely. The question really is, is it not possible to use vibrational aspects to overcome this challenge to the planet?

KIT: Okay then, would laser beams, laser light come under the head of vibration?

INDIRA: Well, they are a very small frequency band of vibration, they won't do it for nuclear wastes.

First, there must be the testing. Second, to have the correct containment while this vibrational testing is being done. Third, to recreate the correct vibrational aspects and then also the testing to be followed in these particular procedures. They will have to be worked out to the exact timing for neutralization to occur. There will be a time element involved in all of this, time is involved in the force that brings these vibrations into attunement.

KIT: And will this all occur within this century?

INDIRA: It depends on whether someone will take it upon themselves to do it. You see, after you put the thought out into the universe, someone will pick it up. What we do from this side is to put out the conceptual force as powerfully as possible and then wait until those that are perceptive pick it up. Frequently, some that are perceptive will pick them up and then discard these concepts. But no matter, we try again.

At my first session with spirit, Chief White Eagle, a Cherokee medicine man, also came through. Chief White Eagle and I would have many subsequent conversations and in addition to his information on the ways of living in balance with the earth forces, he would enter for the purpose of sending the healing sounds through the channel.

CHIEF WHITE EAGLE: I only come to help to prepare this channel and to give you much peace and calm. Of importance is the understanding of Mother Earth. You are to continue to develop this understanding and to spread it to many, for this is one aspect of the Godhead.

You are to garner knowledge of the life of plants, of those things that are edible upon your earth plane. It is not so difficult to learn and if you wish, you will be given assistance. You will learn about the herbs, the feathers, and also the sacred symbols and signs. Permit these to be absorbed, to be thought about, to be given much credence as they occur and are given to you.

Permit all of the signs not only to be understood with the mind, but to be understood by the soul, for this is of major importance. It is important to have a knowledge of Mother Earth, and to know how to live in balance with her.

Upon this realm all from the Indian Nations live in harmony, and there are many that surround you from all Indian Nations. They walk with you and they will join in even greater force as you go about your path.

KIT: Now that I know about the earth shift that will take place in the not-too-distant future, as I've been told, I would like to see that. I would like to be here for it.

I think this can only be described as arrogant bravado, as I am not at all sure I want to be around when this occurs. Actually, for me it is a yes-and-no situation. It is bound to be frightening, but afterwards . . . what an opportunity. Maybe the long yearned for Brotherhood of Man will come to pass and this I would really like to experience.

CHIEF WHITE EAGLE: I am not certain that this is true, that you would like to be here when this occurs. But nevertheless, what is the truth is that you have already begun to shift. It is a gradualness, and it can be as gradual or as sudden as is necessary. There is still a determination to be made as to how sudden it is to be in order to cleanse in the greatest manner.

KIT: How will the determination be made?

CHIEF WHITE EAGLE: Upon the consciousness of man.

KIT: How will mankind get the message?

CHIEF WHITE EAGLE: It is not that you will get the message, it is that you will *put forth* the message. From within yourselves you will determine what it is that you wish to do to assist the planet and to help each other and to know of the oneness. And the more in which you have already learned this, the more in which you have already begun so to serve, the less harsh and sudden will be the shift. So it comes from within the consciousness of man.

I want to talk to you of the preservation of the seeds. Although it has not always been in our capabilities to do this, you now have the knowledge to so do. If there are seeds that have been left for long periods and must be revitalized, you can do this putting an orange light upon them gradually, slowly. Several applications per day for two to three days. Also to let those that are of the highest vibrations that surround you to be with the seeds, to recharge them in much the same way that you would recharge the body. It is most important to have this information because it will be necessary at times in the future to use those seeds that have been kept or stored for some periods of time. And so it will be essential for you to know how to have the highest vitality before you plant. It will also be necessary to give some preparation to the ground that you are putting them in, a vitalization of the soil. This will be done either through the sun or the application of natural lights. And it must be done with some intensity to be effective.

White Eagle goes on to describe how this is to be done. They must be stored beneath the ground, as near to totally dry as possible, in containers shaped like a pyramid but stored upside down. He says that the light to restore the seed can be either the light of the sun, orange filters, or glass, or even the strong orange acetates now in existence, and is to be administered regularly, two to three times daily for best results, not to touch the seeds directly, rather to use the light above the seeds, passing it back and forth over them.

He goes on to remind us that we must not only prepare the soil carefully but must also remember always to plant in the rhythms of the cycles. This, he says, is ancient knowedge, but is often ignored at this time.

Again, you must remember, he says, how to use seeds and the plants thereof for sustenance and nourishment. Seeds will be ground to make various cakes and pastes that will be palatable for those who survive.

KIT: When you speak of the coming earth shift, is it in the near future?

CHIEF WHITE EAGLE: There will be many moons and many suns to come up. We do see it within the next fifteen to twenty years, but only God Himself knows for absolute certainty.

KIT: And we'll be in a position of having to save and look for food?

CHIEF WHITE EAGLE: Not only food, but you will need to preserve knowledge. You will need to preserve items to use. You will need to preserve that which is of benefit for others and for the continuation of humanity itself, for those who are left will have the awesome responsibility of restoring and rebuilding what some would call civilization, to the planet.

To be entrusted with restoring civilization to the planet is not only awesome, it's downright scary. Being as I am, a lifelong romantic, I visualize a planet looking much as it must have in this country before we came along. When we, the European types came to this gloriously beautiful continent a long time ago, we found living here an indigenous people, people living in perfect harmony with nature, and thus by extension, with God. Well, said our ancestors, we can't have this, we must point out to these ignorant savages how misguided they are. Harmony in nature is something we have not experienced and therefore it must be suspect.

So we set about first off by showing them, the ignorant savages, that their spiritual beliefs and practices were wrong, in fact, they were very bad. Their Great Spirit bore no relation to our own beliefs, so we began to persecute them, to shoot them, eventually to force them to send their children away to schools where they would be shown our way, all these terrible acts, mind you, in the name of the white man's God. This in spite of the fact that we had not then, nor have we now, settled amongst ourselves on the best ways to reach God. There are many shouting from the TV pulpits every day and night, to tell us just how we must pursue our paths to righteously come to God, each one of these ministers of God's word preaching a different version of the right path. To each his own, I say, and please let's try not to kill so many of us with our constant warring, also waged in the name of the Prince of Peace. It's a crazy world, isn't it?

So I think of a land of peace among all people, where all are free to live as seems best to them, only taking care not to harm others. Where we will be able to practice whatever form of worship we prefer, just as was intended by those who wrote our constitution, and which has long since been cast aside by those who make the rules for us now.

I envision a future where it will be brother helping brother, with all of us aware of the responsibility of caring for the others, and maybe, just maybe, a planet of peaceful and loving friendship will come into being.

CHAPTER EIGHT

Spiritual Service

ALTHOUGH I'VE ALWAYS BEEN on the side of the oppressed, my involvement with the cause of homeless people really began in the autumn of 1982, a period during which I often walked with my dog on Cabrillo Boulevard here in Santa Barbara.

Cabrillo Boulevard borders the Pacific Ocean, being separated from the beach by a narrow strip of grass where enough palm trees stand to have given it the name of Palm Park. On the other side of the boulevard there is a fairly heavy growth of bushes and as I wrote in the opening chapter, morning after morning, I would see men and women emerging from those bushes, shaking their heads, running fingers through their hair, obviously trying as best they could to neaten themselves before going into town to find a meal.

It has always been hard for me to make eye contact with another human being and not acknowledge his/her presence. It might only be "Hi," but at the very least, I smile. There used to be an older street person here in Santa Barbara, his trademark a long white beard, and I would often pass him and give a greeting. One morning as I walked past where he sat on one of the benches in the little park, he called out to me, "You know, Lady, I'd rather look at your beautiful dog than at a beautiful woman," referring to my shiny coated sheltie, Max. I laughed, made some rejoinder and continued walking. When I returned that way, he called to me again, asking me to come over and sit down and talk with him for a little. Not wanting particularly to join him, I pleaded that I had to be somewhere else in a few minutes, but then he said to me: "How do you ever expect to learn anything about people unless you sit and talk with them?"

That was too provocative a question to be ignored, so of course I did as he asked. He spoke about his past life, his ex-wife, various and sundry topics, then inquired if he could ask me a question. I said sure, and so he asked how old I was. I said it was a question I sidestepped if I could, so then he wanted me to guess his age, which I did. When I started to leave, I asked him how old he thought I was. He said, "Oh, about fifty." I laughed again, and said "Well, I was once." Whereupon he broke out laughing and called after me: "I made you feel good, didn't I?" He was plainly tickled with the encounter and I must admit, so was I. Often have I thought about him and his provocative question, and wondered where he disappeared to, as that was the last time I ever saw him around town.

As I continued my routine walks on Cabrillo Boulevard, I couldn't help thinking about these obviously homeless people, and one day, while talking with my friend Richard, who besides being the executive director of my foundation, has advised me on numerous subjects, I asked him what he thought I could do to help on the homeless issue. It was the fall of 1982, and the problem had not really surfaced as a nationwide issue, let alone a local Santa Barbara problem. Looking back on it now, I realize that a large part of my motivation to help the homeless people came from a desire to involve myself in an issue which had been so important to John Tomson and one on which he had worked so successfully in his own home town of Denver.

Richard Parker has always proven to be a remarkable source of information for me. I asked him once how it happened that he had such a wide diversity of knowledge. He replied that he had been a voracious reader all of his life and that he remembered everything he had ever read and as usual, he had a good suggestion on the question of the homeless. He advised me to call a mutual friend at the University of California at Santa Barbara, a professor of sociology, and discuss it with him.

I did this, asking if he thought one of his graduate students might be interested in doing a survey of the homeless here. He replied that he was sure such a person could be found, and asked what the purpose of the survey would be. I didn't really know except that I felt that if the problem were to be pinpointed, it would be easier to come up with a solution and that I would be interested in funding this person to do the research.

Soon afterwards, I received a call from Robert Rosenthal, who was to be the first of the many friends I would make on this new journey. Rob is a doctoral candidate at UCSB in the field of sociology, in addition to being a talented instrumentalist and composer of witty satirical political songs. He had already been involved with local politics for some years so it was easy to engage his interest in the project. Rob and I met several times so that he could give me a picture of how he planned to proceed. He then began interviewing countless men and women, recording conversations, covering sheets of paper, getting to know the people and the circumstances of their lives, and, in general, doing whatever it is that sociologists do to go about compiling information and statistics.

At that time, and to a large extent even now, the growing number of street people tended to gather under the widely spreading branches of Santa Barbara's Moreton Bay Fig Tree, long a local landmark. There is a small grassy area around the base of this magnificent tree and its root structure is unique in extending several feet above the ground, forming crevices and canyons which can easily cradle a person's body, particularly when softened by a sleeping bag or blanket. Rob spent a lot of time there getting to know "The Fig Tree People" as they've been called—usually in a derogatory tone—and after awhile he brought Nancy Macreadie to meet me.

Nancy is a remarkable woman in her thirties, strong, intelligent, courageous, and one for whom I have tremendous respect. She was living in her old camper with her lover "Protest Bob," as he is known on the street, and, subsequently, their new baby daughter, Crystal Freedom, as well as her seven year old son by her former marriage. Through her indomitable spirit and her organizing talents, Nancy gave the homeless Fig Tree People a sense of belonging. When you're out on the street with no home, no job, an ever-present feeling of anxiety, and in a town where you are consistently harrassed by the law, to have a feeling of belonging can become all important.

Nancy herself had a job, has always worked even while living on the street, and Bob has enough skills so that he often worked as well. This being basically a book on metaphysical wisdom, I will say here that according to my beliefs, Nancy has been given—or has chosen it, rather—a large share of challenges to overcome in this lifetime. As I believe we choose these trials, these opportunities for "the shining of our souls," as Indira Latari puts it, I look at Nancy and see a stalwart spirit learning the lessons she was sent to learn in this lifetime. Although I was by this time deeply engrossed both in my work with spirit as well as with putting together this book, I was irresistibly drawn into the work with the homeless.

Two weeks before Christmas, 1984, I called a friend who is one of the local clergy asking if he would meet with Rob and me to discuss the possibility of encouraging the clergy of Santa Barbara to talk about the situation of the homeless people from their pulpits. It seemed to me that not enough news coverage was being given to this problem and that the clergy had a spiritual obligation to work on it. My friend agreed to make some calls, and I contacted another clergyman who also agreed to meet with us. We had about a dozen people when we met for lunch, including some lay people, some homeless people and one or two business people.

From this meeting grew the Inter-Religious Task Force, and it in turn put together a coalition of churches who assumed the task of giving shelter and food to the homeless people for a set period of time. They have done an outstanding job, and now, as I write this four years later, there exists Transition House, a recently-opened shelter to take the place of the temporary shelter which the churches have provided.

Looking back at the unfolding of the past four years, both the humor and the irony of that meeting strike me. We were a dedicated group of sincere people, gathered together to make known to the local clergy the dire needs of the homeless. In a sense, that first meeting spawned an interest in the plight of the homeless here in Santa Barbara—this being the hometown of our current president Ronald Reagan—which ultimately helped focus national media attention on the problem. One of the little ironies in view of what was to unfold, was that to accomplish this meeting I had asked for and received advice from Indira Latari. In other words, I received guidance from the invisible world through a trance channel to apply to a very desperate real-world situation which was confronting communities across the land.

KIT: I've organized a meeting today directed towards helping solve the plight of the homeless here in Santa Barbara. There will be twelve people present, more or less, a Catholic priest, an Episcopalian minister, a Unitarian minister, a few of the homeless people and some business people. And I'm hoping that there will be some positive suggestions and means for putting them in practice coming from this meeting. Do you foresee a positive result?

INDIRA: Certainly. The principal thing to keep in mind, perhaps, with these particular persons, is that some will be more action-oriented than others, and you should take advantage of this. Talking is fine, but whenever there is a suggestion made for some specific action, even if it doesn't fully resolve it, try to elaborate on this and let any suggestion of "this can't be done," etc., go by the way. You see?

KIT: Yes, of course.

INDIRA: It's all right to listen, and you will need a little sorting of "this doesn't work" etc. But eventually, you will have a start toward specific action.

KIT: That's what we need, specific action towards getting a shelter for these homeless people. At least for some of them. Obviously we can't do it all, help everyone.

INDIRA: Remember what we've already told you, that you may not have one specific shelter because it will be too much, too many would be against having so many of the homeless people gathered in any one neighborhood. If there's too much congregation of the homeless it might be construed as harmful, and so the fearful people would become more fearful. The meeting will be valuable because their needs must be identified, and it will be found that some can be assisted so that they no longer have to be homeless people.

Indira went on to "sort them out." Some, she felt, don't really want to be helped, they have chosen and enjoy their life of freedom, difficult though it may be. Those people often seek and take jobs where a little money will be made, enough to satisfy the needs and desires of the moment. Others may not be able to be assisted at this particular time as far as making themselves self-sufficient goes. There will be no homogencity here, she warned, and that fact must be understood by those of us seeking to help with this national problem.

Our conversation then turned not only to the lack of shelters for the homeless, but the lack of low cost housing of any sort, where a person with a few dollars can go for shelter. Not much—if anything—is available, not only for the actual homeless people who live here in Santa Barbara, but for those passing through on their way elsewhere. Indira added a few comments on the necessity for rules limiting the stay of homeless people, due, of course, to the scarcity of beds.

KIT: I see what you're saying, Indira. With so few beds available for any homeless people, permanent or transient, it's important that time limits must be set. Unfortunately! I think it's hard for residents of a city to realize that many of their fellow citizens are literally without any place to live. The popular notion seems to be that they have come here from all over the country and chosen this city because of its climate, the ocean, and the pleasant atmosphere.

INDIRA: It's not a popular cause because it is so misunderstood. We've already told you this, but you need to do some educating, and educating is very difficult because those that are in the power positions have a stronghold on keeping old popular notions going, not wanting the slightest change. They keep alive notions like, "If they (the homeless) wanted to, they could help themselves."

KIT: Or, that they're all mentally deficient, or alcoholics and shouldn't be free on the streets at all.

INDIRA: Well, there are some of those. There are also those that really can help themselves, but they've gotten to a point where things have gone badly for them for so long that they become afraid to go out and seek work. You see, you have a certain percentage now, approximately twenty per cent in your city that are homeless because of certain economic conditions, factories, mines, automobile plants, endless closings of work places. These people have not chosen to be homeless. Then there is another percentage which is perhaps somewhat larger who are on the streets because they have chosen it, believe it or not.

I agreed with Indira when she went on to say that these differences within the homeless themselves must be pointed out. She explained that it might be a question of "values" for the ones being asked to give money towards feeding and housing those with no shelters. Many might be willing to support the mentally ill, the disabled, those out of work because of an economy over which they have no control. But sadly, a homeless person who falls under these qualifications looks no different from her/his brother or sister who chooses to seek this lifestyle because "I prefer to sleep under the stars," as one man recently told me. So this last person lies around under the Fig Tree—along with others whose needs and wants are entirely different—but regardless, all of them get sent to jail in Santa Barbara because they are all sleeping "under the stars," a misdemeanor in this fair city, whether it is their wish or not. According to one recent statistic, the city spent over a quarter of a million dollars in 1985 prosecuting these homeless people for the simple "crime" of sleeping outside. This decision was challenged by a local judge who pointed out that to be consistent the city must then arrest all children for example, who might sleep in their back yards on a summer night, as well as lovers spending a romantic night together on the beach, and so on. It reminded me of my younger daughter who as a child considered it the height of joy to sleep out in a tree not far from the house, where a treehouse had been built, a platform really, and where she and a friend could spread a sleeping bag and spend an uncomfortble night in the tree.

Indira pointed out that the biggest help that can be given will be to those who are there because they've lost their grip, so to speak, on the ability to obtain employment.

INDIRA. They can't get out of it because if they want to take a job position, the potential employer will want to know where to reach them, and well, what are they going to say, since they have no home, none of your little boxes for communications, you see? No one can reach them to discuss the job possibility.

KIT: Well, that's exactly what we're trying to arrange now in this project, where there will be a 24-hour telephone with volunteers to handle it, and so the homeless person can apply for the job and say, "I can be reached at this number," and also at this same place with the telephone, to be able to give out vouchers so they can go to the laundromat or to the Salvation Army for showers. Even better, of course, would be to have a place not only with telephones, but with showers and toilets as well, and a waiting room where people can sit while waiting for a call, and for their clothes if there could be a washing machine and dryer there, too.

INDIRA: That's quite correct. Now, remember that this is only a percentage of the persons, and if you want to reach for the monetary in the community, you can perhaps get some support for that notion, you see. But you need to label it differently, perhaps, than as a homeless project because they may not want to give to that under that name. Perhaps if you can call it Economic Bootstrap, or persons being assisted to help themselves, that's fine. You understand, that is your American way as it stands.

Another thing to understand is that if someone has been on your streets for ten years, or even two years, and they are given the opportunity to change their way of life, they will be so frightened, so absolutely frightened to alter it, you have no idea of what you are suggesting, in some respects. They have become accustomed to that.

I'm sure that is true. They know a certain security in being where they are, have made friends in that street environment, and to leave that familiarity, that tiny familiar something in their otherwise frightening, threatening world, may well be beyond their capacity.

INDIRA: It's similar to taking a very nice-appearing lady, one who's educated, and has spent all her life raising her family, assisting her mate, but the family is no longer there, you see? Now there is an opportunity for her to try out her wings in a different way, outside the confines of the family, and she's frightened.

KIT: Of course, that has to be true.

INDIRA: Most will not appear, however, to be frightened, because they're wearing their outer trappings, that would make them look as confident no?

KIT: Yes, it's as if they wore suits of armor. I see what you're saying, Indira, that they have their fears about being able to return to the regular world, just as the woman who's been a homemaker, etc., has about re-entering the workaday world. It's something I might bring up at this meeting, we're going to brainstorm about the many different aspects of the problem.

INDIRA: You will also need to have some person-to-person contact between a person who doesn't live on the street with one who does.

KIT: We're trying to do that, too. And some of the homeless will be there today, as a matter of fact.

INDIRA: Yes, that will be most beneficial. But I'm speaking about when you start the process of assisting in which there will be someone that says they have so much time to devote to talking with another person, just to talk about the problems they may not wish to raise with someone who just sits and answers their phones, or who comes and goes . . . there is a need to make a tighter connection with one person, you see?

KIT: I know what you mean, Indira. It's like learning the importance of even the most minimal human contact. Like walking down the street and making eye contact with another person, then saying hello, strictly a human-to-human thing. It's like nothing and everything wrapped in one package.

I recently heard someone quote one of the homeless people saying that quite often he feels like a *non*-person, seeing other people avert their heads as if they can not bear the sight of the homeless person. This man asked if the other humans had any idea how it felt to be totally ignored, to be treated as though one did not exist. I have wondered about that myself, about what is going on inside the head of the man we are afraid to speak to, the one we are afraid to acknowledge as another human being. What can be any more important than a human-to-human contact or more chilling to the soul than the opposite, a total rejection of one's inherent and *un*alienable humanity?

INDIRA: Well, we want to tell you something as far as your homeless are concerned. Most valuable to provide assistance, first. Second, even more valuable to provide what you call teaching, for unless you do this, you're not providing as high an opportunity as is possible.

It is always correct to feed those that are hungry, for example. The good must do this, for when one is hungry it is as if you were feeding God. However, when you continue to feed and to feed and to feed the same persons, when they do not also garner greater understandings along with it, it is only one level of help. But it is an even higher level of help when it is that the opportunities are given for the homeless, the hungry and others, to grow. Opportunity to grow in their own self understanding, to grow in their understanding of their connection with God, to grow in their understanding of their purpose upon the earth plane.

It does not mean that you must stand there personally and teach, but it is true that the opportunities need to be given to show them how they can prosper, how they can shelter themselves, and how they can become, how do you call this, able to feed themselves. Do you understand this?

KIT: Yes, I do.

Indira went on to urge me to teach, or show, the homeless how they can help themselves to grow, to better their situations so as not to continually be in this desperate state for the rest of their lives. She emphasized that it is of course possible that even with the best of efforts and intentions, there is no guarantee that they will not at some future time again find themselves back on the street, but points out always, that they are responsible for their own lives, that they themselves can make the changes needed and urges them to do so. Indira stresses always the need for *inner growth*, not only for the homeless themselves, but for those in the community who can help in these problems.

During those particular conversations on the topic of this devastatingly important social problem, Indira charged me with the responsibility to "educate those in the community" who are able to help with the homeless, and to try to share with them the great need for understanding and compassion.

In the work here in Santa Barbara on the homeless problem, there have been times of great victory, few and far between but nonetheless significant. At the Legal Defense Center, a non-profit law office dedicated to poverty law and social justice, Willard Hastings, the attorney at the Center, fought for and won the voting rights for the homeless, a right which had been denied by local officials with the excuse that a person without a home had no right to vote. This was felt to be an important decision with statewide and national repercussions.

Of course, the disappointments have come, too. Willard has recently been trying to have the "Go to sleep, go to jail" law, as it is referred to by the victims of the law, rescinded, and had hoped it might be argued in front of the Supreme Court—a few days ago, however, the news came that the court had refused to hear the case. So for the people here in Santa Barbara with no place to lay their heads at night, it's back to police harrassment, and endless nights in jail. As few ever have the money for the fines, most have to work out their sentences working for the city. It appears to me that we have been chipping away, chipping away for a long time, and although I do have my moments of discouragement, it is true that we have made a pretty fair amount of progress, too.

INDIRA: There will always be those upon the planet that do not have shelter. There will always be those upon your planet that are hungry. And it is most correct to help both of them, as best you can. But the manner in which you do it is most important—for if you give them only a shelter without greater understanding, well, you're not assisting them in the same vein as you can if you provide the shelter and expansion of who they are.

It is important to teach others in the community this, as well. First, the compassion, yes, for other human beings. And, second, the aspect of expanding. When it is that you permit others also to assist in this project, they must know of the importance of expansion of each individual, as well as the need to feed, house and shelter those in need. When others participate, it grows, and they will grow in their own understanding. They will grow in their own selflessness. They will grow in their coming to grips with who they are, see?

KIT: Do you mean those who are helping to establish a shelter?

INDIRA: Both, they and those who need the shelter. The cooperative effort has already been begun. Very good. Expand upon this now in manners which will touch the hearts and the pursestrings of many. See? Igniting is most appropriate. And then the igniting of the teaching aspects.

KIT: Well, Indira, would you think it would be a good thing to have once a week or every two weeks—as I do at my home—such a meeting downtown, accessible to the homeless? And tell people if they want to come, sit and talk, that there will be a time and a place for it?

INDIRA: It would of course be quite different from the gathering which meets in your home. You will find that their consciousnesses are starting at an altogether different place. Do you understand?

KIT: Hmmmmm.

INDIRA: You see, those that come to your home are in all varieties and shades. Among them are some who do not really trust that they can have happiness, that they can have a certain level of earthly goods, that they can move on and let go, that they can have greater calm and peacefulness. They will test it with their little toes, see? Those that you would find without shelter have even greater fear because they, above all, can't believe that they could have beyond what they have now, which is next to nothing.

KIT: Yes, and yet I'm sure there are many of them who are aware that they can change their situations, that they do have control over their own lives.

INDIRA: Yes, they will know in their hearts, but they won't almost dare to believe it. And, of course, that is one of the reasons why they are where they are.

KIT: If I understand you clearly, Indira, what you're saying is that they have so little sense of self worth that they don't think they're worthy of having any happiness?

INDIRA: It isn't just a question of self-worth, although that is a portion of it. But there is also a portion of a lack of self-worth among those that come to your house for discussion. It is just a question of degree for some persons. Or, there is a negativity there, an old sadness, or an incapacity of one kind or another where they do not really believe they can come beyond the incapacity.

KIT: Yes, I agree with you on that. Well, do you think it would be a good idea to have this kind of discussion group amongst some of the homeless people I know?

INDIRA: You will find, how do you call it?, a mixed reaction. You'll find experimentation interesting for yourself.

KIT: So you're saying it would be a good idea to try it and see what happens?

INDIRA: Yes, but you will get a mixed result.

KIT: But it doesn't really matter so much, the result. . .

INDIRA: The process can be extremely important to you to understand what is really there, so to speak.

KIT: It will teach me a lot, of that I have no doubt.

INDIRA: What will be most interesting is to permit persons from the community, whether those that have no homes and those that do have homes, those that have no positions and those that do have positions, to intermingle. Because they all want in their heart of hearts to have love, acceptance, closeness. See? All human beings have that commonality of desire. And most important, they're all connected with God, whether or not they admit it.

KIT: I hope I'll be guided if I do this group, as to how to approach them, because it will have to be a little bit of a different approach from the meeting which is held at my house. But I suspect the homeless would like to have such a place to come and talk.

INDIRA: We want to tell you to see the consciousness, to stand there with a blank slate and permit the emergence of the consciousness, the emergence of the awareness, of the capabilities, the spirituality of each and every individual with whom you come into contact. That's where we're most interested. Yes, they have to have a place to put their heads—because before there is a place to put their heads, they find it difficult, challenging, to move closer to God. But it is all very subtle. Transformation is subtle, see? You have an opportunity to show transformation in all kinds of settings: in your prisons, on the streets, etc.

KIT: Well, Indira, would it be good, would it be of help to them to do a bit as I do in my own house? To ask people how they feel about their lives, to ask, for example, if they see any changes coming in their lives, and if they do, how would the change come about, through themselves, or through outside agencies. If they will explore such questions it will put them in touch with themselves in a way that is perhaps new for them.

INDIRA: Of course, but you will have to do a different type of pump priming, because you will not want to entertain only negativity. You will not want to entertain only complaints. You will simply want to dig a little deeper which may take a little bit of shaking out to do, see?

We want to tell you something else: the idea of the shelter is a good one, but it is also for them to raise their consciousness to assist in the building and the construction of the facility, and the caring for it, also.

KIT: Yes, that would be wonderful.

INDIRA: When you only give to someone, it's good, but when you give them the opportunity to expand, you're giving them more. When you're giving them the opportunity to reach inward toward the God within, you're giving them the ultimate. That's the ultimate that you can do, is to give someone the understanding of who they are and who they are in conjunction with God. It does not mean that they're only to sit in the lotus position and pray. No, no, they must still continue on with their lives, must still dedicate to their understanding. To commit each to the other, see?

What Indira is telling me applies equally to the friends who come to my house for our Saturday gatherings, people whose lives are dramatically different from those of the homeless. Low self-esteem is apparently universal, regardless of life situation. Rich, poor, white middle class, black, brown poorer classes, it doesn't matter, we all seem to have difficulty in believing, really and truly believing, that we deserve love and caring from others. Why? How to go about that gigantic task of education? To reach inside, as Indira says, to get to know ourselves. How to describe this progress? Impossible. Each of us knows in our hearts what we need to do to continue the upward struggle.

INDIRA: Incidentally, in discussions about understanding, it does not mean that you do not feed and give shelter when and where possible. Create those aspects in which persons will open their homes to those with no home. So, go forward in letting them know about one-to-one communication. You have seen concrete evidence of progress towards sheltering the homeless by the churches so continue to spread the word of compassion for the needy.

KIT: Indira, just this morning on the local television I heard one of the ministers involved with the work sheltering the homeless, taking the credit for it. And, indeed, he seems to be getting all the credit from the community. A little feeling of resentment goes through me because until I called him last year to suggest that he get the clergy together to work on this problem to the best of my knowledge this had not been done in the churches in any concerted effort. Now that it's become a reality, my colleague Rob and I are ignored because we're involved with The Fig Tree People. The religious group was careful to mention in print that they were in no way connected with those people. And as that little feeling of resentment went through me this morning I thought, "Well, that's ridiculous, what difference does it make whether or not he gives me or Rob any credit."

INDIRA: It makes a lot of difference. Let me tell you why it makes a difference. It is part of what we're speaking of, the learning process that all persons, even those that call themselves ministers unto God, all persons must learn. All consciousnesses need expansion, never doubt that. And so, it is to call it to their attention, see?

KIT: I would find it difficult to do that. There is a part of me that would like to, but it would be difficult for me to do that.

INDIRA: Yes, but that is a part of your learning process, not to let anything sink below the surface but just to put it above the surface. For it isn't a question of getting any of the credit, it's a question of teaching other persons. It's a question of teaching them that there are all levels of persons involved with the homeless problem. There needs to be much education. For example, you could have a one-to-one program, Adopt-a-Street-Person, see?

KIT: Adopt-a-Street-Person?

INDIRA: Yes!

KIT: That's a good slogan, isn't it?

INDIRA: Well, maybe not so much speaking of it literally, but we're speaking of the opportunity to coach, to assist, and to turn loose. That is the greatest. When you have taught them, then turn them loose.

KIT: Yes, I learned that a long time ago, the way to keep people is to always let them go.

INDIRA: Unfortunately, not all understand this. On the question of the homeless, ignite. The biggest utilization of the monetary is to ignite persons into the understanding, the understanding of the seriousness of the problem, of the part they can and must play. This you do first by demonstration to others, secondly, by permitting them to have access and communications with the homeless ones, not to have fear of them.

KIT: Yes, certainly, but how though? It's a very difficult thing.

INDIRA: Well, you have been creative before, no?

I have learned a lot since working with the homeless and as I recently began a new project with them, I expect to learn a great deal more. As of this writing, the Catholic Social Service people are letting us use a room for two hours on alternate Tuesday afternoons and word has been passed around that any of the street people interested can come and share their feelings, their thoughts, and themselves with each other at those times. This is strictly a personal discussion group, not organizational nor political in any way.

So far we have met only twice. The first time only one young man showed up, a very interesting, highly spiritual person, and as he now has found a job I don't expect him to return since we meet during working hours. At the second meeting, six or seven men came—four of them were seriously destitute, plagued not only by their homelessness and lack of work, but by alcoholism and drug addiction as well, while the other two could be described in the same way as the young man from the first meeting, very spiritually oriented and very thoughtful, though still driven by the same problems as the others. Both of them were in their twenties.

One of the young men that afternoon was extremely angry. He was angry with society, with the government, with everything about his world as he sees it, and of course, most of all, angry with himself, although he wasn't aware of that. He interests me and I will be disappointed if he stays away from the next meeting. When I asked him how he sees his life, how he would change it if he could, he said it was impossible in this society to change it and cited several reasons for this unwillingness to move from his present psychological and psychic position. He said the best change he could think of was to go out to the end of the pier and "take swimming lessons."

SPIRITUAL SERVICE   157

There is no question that all of the men present that day are alcoholics in one form or another. The subject was discussed and all admitted to being addicted. The angry man said that a bottle helped if you were trying to sleep in a phone booth on a cold, rainy night.

One of the men spoke of the lack of nutritional value in the food they receive, and although it can be argued that this only shows ingratitude for what they are given, I have heard the same comment made about prison food: the sameness, the starchiness, the lack of fresh vegetables and fruit. I have thought about this and often wonder how these homeless people can have as much spirit as they do, considering the many problems they struggle with. So: no sleep without constant interruptions and harrassment from the police, no health giving food, and you have a set of discouraging problems unknown to those of us still living at home.

Many years ago when I was nineteen and newly married, I was asked to canvass for the United Way campaign in a very poor district called the Irish Channel in the city of New Orleans where I lived at the time. It was a lesson for me, one I never forgot. My lesson that day was that the poor understand the needs of the poor. This message came loud and clear from every house I approached. The housewife might take down from a high shelf the coffee can where she kept her money, maybe fish out a fifty cent piece, or perhaps half of that, and holding it out to me would apologize for its being so small a sum but that she knew how great the need was for even the smallest contribution. Not one woman turned down my request. They knew first hand how badly someone else might need that quarter.

The following year I was given a "big donors" list, and one of my aunts pledged the handsome sum of twenty five dollars. This aunt had told us the previous Christmas Eve at my grandparents' annual family dinner, that her husband, my uncle, had given her a diamond necklace for Christmas. She sighed and said, "I guess he forgot that I already have one." Another lesson! The rich have no conception of the needs of the poor, and in general, have no desire to find out.

There have been two homeless men murdered while sleeping here within the past few months. The killer of the first has never been found. The killer of the second homeless person is a young man attending a privately-run military school. He is from a well-to-do Palo Alto family, and was acquitted of first degree murder, and only found guilty of manslaughter, after he publicly confessed to numerous stab attacks on the victim. Then to make it final, the comfortably-fed and housed boarding school student slit the homeless man's throat while the victim, a transient, was imploring, "No, friend, no."

An official high in the city administration said that had the homeless man been obeying the law, i.e. not sleeping in public (the twenty-nine year old victim had been lying peacefully in his bedroll, listening to his radio, in a little bandstand in the middle of a deserted public park) he would not have been killed. His killer told the court that he and a prep school friend had been looking for Latinos as they "thought" some Mexicans had been bothering friends of theirs. The victim, by the way, was an Anglo.

KIT: Yes, I think a lot of people are learning about the homeless from the churches' programs right now. The volunteers, I mean, that work with the homeless through various church organizations and groups.

INDIRA: Correct, but some of this could be brought to further light by bringing it into the open. You're a catalyst, you understand how to use aspects of bringing forth into the light.

KIT: I'll have to give it some thought. I'm sure it would be a good thing to do, no doubt about that.

INDIRA: Lighting the flame. That is what your life really is about, lighting the flame in different forms and manners. See? That is what you're doing in your writing. That is what you do when you speak with persons on an individual basis. That is what you're doing when you're meeting with persons and they're congregating, and you're encouraging them.

I recently lighted a different kind of flame when I permitted myself to be interviewed by a national magazine in which I expressed my feelings about the way the city and county authorities have handled the homeless problem. The mayor told me that I should apologize publicly to the city and defended her thesis of the great things the city has done, and is doing for the homeless.

The Santa Barbara Legal Defense Center had invited Mitch Snyder, the national advocate for the homeless in Washington,D.C., to come here and address those who wanted to hear him. I was asked by the organization if I would put up the money for Snyder's trip which I agreed to do. As a result I received a lot of criticism because of the confrontation which followed. I could readily understand the mayor's wrath but when she told me she thought I owed the city a public apology, I thought it a bit much to make me the scapegoat. And that very event proved to be the thing that brought the plight of the homeless people in Santa Barbara to the attention of the nation.

Rob Rosenthal and I recently had a long interview with Her Honor in which I told her that I had asked for the meeting in the hope that we could sit down together and come to enough of a degree of understanding so that we could work together on the problem. At this writing I have hopes that this will happen.

That day was an interesting one with great contrasts. It began, as I just wrote, with the interview at City Hall, where the problems of the immediate present were the topic of discussion. It ended that night at Verna Yater's where there was a meeting being recorded by a professional video crew of a group channeling session. At this meeting we had been asked to bring questions relating to particular topics, one of which was extra-terrestrials. So in one day I went from a meeting with the mayor at City Hall to discuss the plight of the homeless here in Santa Barbara, to an evening of discussion on outer space—somewhat dizzying perhaps, but very interesting.

John Donne's statement, made a few hundred years ago, still applies: " . . . any man's death diminishes me because I am involved in all Mankind. . ." Our spiritual work is as apparent now as when those words were written as we are indeed, all of us, involved with all mankind.

And it was of course, Christ who said "Inasmuch as ye have done it to the least of these ye have done it unto me."

CHAPTER NINE

Extraterrestrials

OVER THE YEARS my interest in spacecraft, space beings, as well as other universes has constantly grown. Indira tells me there are universes beyond universes so far undreamed of by man.

I can remember sitting in my car one day by the ocean, listening to the waves and thinking about the beginning and the end of this universe that we occupy. At that time, I had no knowledge of the concept of universes beyond ours. And though I realize that trying to grasp even a faint glimmer of such a subject is more than a challenge, nevertheless I'm sure many of you have had similar moments of contemplation.

There were fractions of seconds when I felt *something* was within my grasp of understanding, but it was quickly followed by frustration, as the glimmer of cosmic understanding faded from my consciousness. Given that I have no knowledge of physics, any glimpse into this other, greater reality, must be purely inituitive.

When I was first reading the Seth books some years ago, the concept of "simultaneity" intrigued me. I have recently experienced sharp little visions which may quite possibly be glimpses into these other, simultaneously lived lives—meaning simply that some part of us is also existing in other bodies on our planet or on others, with each life paralleling this one. As I understand this concept, it means that our spirit, our soul, which is the real self in my belief, is capable of living in more

160

than one body at the same time. There are parts of the soul which make up the whole and thus we may be capable of glimpsing our "other realities" at times.

I have always felt that time, as such, does not exist, that it is something that we made up, as evidenced by the complex calendars invented by the Mayans, the Chinese and other peoples who evolved methods of keeping track of our lives. Indira frequently mentions this very thing, saying that time on her side of the veil is quite different from how those of us still in our bodies perceive it. I recently heard a man on TV speak of light as "defining time for us."

A friend in Phoenix has given me several books on the subject of UFOs, all with seemingly well-documented information including photographs of spacecraft coming in for landing, hovering, and a number of the photos also show people standing on the ground watching. My friend, a well-respected journalist and labor organizer, has also told me that some years ago, when he lived in northern New Mexico in a remote mountainous area, he frequently saw spacecraft landing and taking off and that a number of residents of this sparsely-populated region had had similar experiences. This concurs with the stories others tell about spacecraft seemingly choosing to appear in sparsely populated mountainous areas. The reasons for choosing such remote areas for contact are many and varied, of course: the vibrations of the particular area, or the reluctance to arouse human anxiety, are but two of the many possible reasons. Through another psychic channel here in Santa Barbara, a space being has been quoted as saying that they wish to disturb our planet and its inhabitants as little as possible. They are fully aware of the affects on humans which their manifestations might generate.

Shirley MacLaine, in her book "Out on a Limb," writes about just such occurrences in the high mountain region of Peru where she was taken by her friend David. She describes two official-looking signs placed by the roadside on the highest mountain pass. One sign announces that this is the highest spot in the world for a railroad train to travel, while the other gives the electrifying news that the very place where you are standing reading the sign is an acknowledged spot for observing low-flying spacecraft. The exact words on the sign, translated from Spanish, are: *Flying Saucers Do Exist: UFO Contact Point.*

Indira told me on more than one occasion that the study of vibrations—whether through physics, metaphysics, or one's inner meditations—will begin the understanding required to give us a broader vision of other beings, whether on other planets, or other planes. According to my spirit teacher, vibratory rates on other planets are quite different from those on our own. Some are quicker, others slower, and so, if we were to step onto another plane or planet, it's perfectly possible, indeed probable, that we wouldn't see the beings there, vibrating at different rates of frequency than our own. I believe this to be entirely true, and frequently have the awareness of the presence, or presences of other beings from other frequencies, although I deeply regret not being able to see them.

It seems that an identical phenomenon occurs whenever spacecraft are near: there are some who will never see them, others who will easily see them, while still others will see them but later deny, even to themselves, that they actually did see a spacecraft or space being. They are not vibrating quite close enough to the beings from outer space. There are some who have been taken aboard spacecraft and who have written about it. Others have *claimed* to have been taken aboard, but in actual fact they have not. Theirs is perhaps a wish for publicity, or maybe a case of simple self-delusion, a wish that it had indeed been so. From the accounts which I've read or heard about, those who have been aboard UFOs have had their bodies prepared through the vibratory aspects necessary for such adjustment. And, from what I understand, this compares to the way in which the body of a channel is prepared so that contact with and communication from spirit can be made.

I have had several discussions with Indira during which the subject of extraterrestrial life came up, including the idea that there may be any number of such beings walking around the planet amongst us. Ruth Montgomery has written about this concept in great depth in her book, *Aliens Among Us*, which I recommend to all seekers of knowledge concerning other realities.

Although I've seen any number of interesting and unexplainable things in the night sky, I had one experience here in Santa Barbara marked indelibly in my consciousness, and so I discussed it with Indira during one of my sessions wherein we talked about extra-terrestrials.

KIT: When I saw a spacecraft myself, about a year and a half ago, it was if all my life I'd been waiting for it. And there it was. I was with two other people, my grandson and his wife, who had come to take me out to supper. I live on the oceanside of the coastal range, and as we reached the bottom of the hill and made the right turn to take us into town, out of nowhere, coming low on the horizon straight towards us, appeared a brilliantly white object. It was completely round, completely encircled with blazing white rays, and was coming straight towards us at windshield level. Stunned, we stopped the car, all exclaiming, "My God!"at the same time. We pulled over to the side of the road as had other cars in front and behind us. It came right at us, almost filling the whole windshield. Suddenly, as if it had encountered a wall, it reversed its course and zoomed directly away into the distance and was gone. Just merged with the sky, it seemed, and always on the same flat horizontal course. This all happened so quickly that the whole incident was over much faster than I can write about it. But there was no doubt in my mind as to what we had seen. When we stopped by the road, I exclaimed: "All my life I've waited for this and here it is!"

INDIRA: You have had a lot of familiarity with it. That was not your first encounter. It was the first one that you would remember upon this particular round, and that is what makes it so profound for you. It is not unlike those who step into other realms, they are absolutely overwhelmed because they have remembered it their whole lives. And so they say, "Here it is!" They have been looking for it, but in the wrong places.

KIT: Well, my grandson turned on the radio and the announcer was saying that people from all over the county were calling in to find out what that thing was in the sky. And that was the only word we ever heard about it, there was nothing in the papers the next day nor on radio or television. It's another example, I suppose, of what a friend calls "fugitive news flashes," the kind you hear only once, with never a follow-up to satisfy your curiosity. We thought the military authorities at Vandenberg Air Force Base just north of here probably gave the order to put a lid on the whole event.

The interesting thing was that my grandson, maybe twenty minutes later, said "Oh, I don't think it was a spacecraft, probably an Air Force rocket or something." He was denying it, of course, not permitting himself to know what he'd seen. But his wife and I both said, "Of course its a spacecraft. There's nothing else it could have been. What other aircraft do you think could have made those radical maneuvers?" Thomas clung to his decision that he had seen a rocket of some sort from the Air Force base and that "everyone knows spaceships don't exist."

INDIRA: The phenomenon you are describing is one that is very familiar. It happens over and over again, the denial after a short period.

KIT: Why is that?

INDIRA: Because it is not in the person's frame of reference or support. You see, if it were to become supported that there is life all around you, life on other planets, that there is communication possible with these other beings, then it would stretch the frame of the individual's perception of reality. And when this happens, the mind sometimes says, "I don't believe it. It wasn't real."

KIT: I think I see what you mean. I don't know if this is a fair question or not, Indira, but I'm wondering where we stand, we earth people, evolution-wise in comparison with those from other planets. Maybe it doesn't even make any sense to ask such a question?

INDIRA: Oh, it is fair, and it might make some sense. Whether it is entirely relevant may be another matter. As to putting it on a scale, I cannot do that because it would be like trying to fit unidentical things on the same scale.

There is not as much evolvement upon this particular planet as there is upon many others, and actually, upon what you call other universes. There are others which are much more evolved than the universe you are finding yourself in at this time. You may ask how does this occur. Well, those that are upon these planetary aspects of earth are here because they must be here. They have not evolved sufficiently to be able to handle it anywhere else.

KIT: Why is that?

INDIRA: All those that are upon the earth plane, that are here because they must be here, are as precious to God as those that are the most evolved teachers to come from other planets to be of assistance. Those come to serve, even though they have evolved to where they could go on, they do not have to be here.

KIT: From a philosophical point of view, this is a question I've thought about a great deal. But when we speak of being evolved, what exactly are we evolving toward?

INDIRA: The full and final return to the Godhead in which there is no separation any more. All is one, completely, totally. You will have glimpses of that at this time.

In reference to Ruth Montgomery's books discussing extraterrestrials walking the earth today, I asked Indira about the purpose and nature of the extraterrestrials' interactions with our planet.

KIT: Indira, are these beings that are visiting our planet coming to teach us?

INDIRA: Some are. They are here to help more than to teach. Again, it is a question of not always being able to interfere or interact with people on your earth, because you and others have chosen this particular planet to have a round upon because there are aspects here from which you can learn. Now, within the next twenty years, there will be dire straits and circumstances and great challenges to planet earth. It is already right now in the stress.

They have been given permission by your hierarchy upon the planet, to be near in the event that they are needed to give more instructions. They are only checking on the conditions of the earth plane at this particular moment. They have not yet done a lot of what you call direct teaching.

KIT: But are they in a position to help us?

INDIRA: Of course. Now, I would tell you this: there are those who have suggested upon your earth that certain individual humans are to be lifted away in these spacecraft. There are no such plans to do this. You had best all be prepared to remain upon the planet as it is now. It does not mean, however, that it is impossible to lift individuals away from the earth plane. That is possible. But it is complex in comparison to other things. If God wishes, there can be direct remaking of certain bodies, and simply having them be back very quickly if there is massive destruction.

You should also realize that there are those who come to your earth without ever having to use a spacecraft. They simply, and not necessarily slowly, alter their vibratory frequencies as they come near to your earth planet and they make contact with those that leave themselves open for this as a possibility.

In *Aliens Among Us*, Ruth Montgomery writes also of space people as "understanding the mysteries of dissolving and reassembling solid matter." Everything being energy, they know how to alter the vibrational patterns and manipulate the atoms. Elsewhere, Indira has spoken about Stonehenge, the Pyramids, and other such gigantic structures as having been assembled in a similar psychic fashion, so to speak. And what about the secrets of the yogis, concerning materializations and dematerializations? It has even been suggested that the master Jesus practiced this secret wisdom (of moving material atoms and molecules with vibrational energies) in many of his miraculous acts on earth. There is much documentation on the eighteen years Jesus spent in India and Egypt, and it is said that there he studied with the master yogis, giving them of his knowledge as he acquired theirs.

A few weeks ago, I went with my friend Jack Underhill, the publisher of *Life Times*, a new magazine devoted to higher consciousness, to a session with another channel here in Santa Barbara. Jack had told me about a young woman Rusty, that she was just beginning to channel, that she'd attended one or two of Verna Yater's classes in opening oneself up to channeling, but that was the extent of Rusty's experience in this dimension. From Jack, I'd also learned that among other entities, Rusty was channeling the consciousness of a being from outer space.

I liked Rusty's vibrations immediately, and found the atmosphere of the house where she was living warm and welcoming. She and her daughter shared the house with her sister Peggy, and Peggy's children, as well as with another woman and her three daughters. The girls were all in their teens, from early to late, and I had the feeling they all loved one another very much, girls and parents, too.

There were perhaps fifteen or more of us there that night and the spirits who were already using Rusty to channel were in evidence. The first one to speak calls himself The Ancient One. He speaks softly and with much wisdom. His words that night were fairly general, which I have noticed is often the case in group readings. It is rare at a group reading that much important information comes out. Often people ask quite personal questions dealing with their own lives, which is most of the time of value only to them.

The Ancient One was followed by a second entity who gave his name as Godfrey. Godfrey is a more contemporary being with a breezy manner. Several of us in the room asked questions which he answered apparently to the satisfaction of his questioners. Godfrey gave extraordinary sounds before leaving us, piercing, exciting, and I couldn't help wondering how the neighbors liked them.

When I went the second time, it was for a private, one-to-one session. Rusty and I talked for a few minutes prior to going into trance. Here's part of my conversation with her.

RUSTY: Well, Godfrey has told us that this is really an important time, as we know. There are many on the other side who desire to experience and to serve and to assist us here now. And so they're coming through, actually learning the mechanics of speaking through channels, as an additional way of reaching humans to make us understand what is happening.

When I had first seen Rusty at the group channeling, I saw a slender, red-haired woman in her thirties, with a vulnerable look about her. However, I was instantly impressed with her energy as she went into trance, feeling that she almost exploded with inner energy and my impression of vulnerability gave way to a recognition of wiry strength. It was an interesting transformation in my feelings about her. As she channeled the various entities, her body was quite mobile, moving in her chair much as I'd witnessed Kevin Ryerson do during his trances. She was quite still while channeling the space being, however, and spoke in a faint, far away voice. My feelings about the vibrations of the Alien were only awe, and it is hard to say how much this was my own wonderment projecting, or if the vibrations were actually more rarified. It was a tremendous experience for me to realize my actual contact with a being from outer space and I had no doubt that a new dimension was being added to my life.

Rusty went on to tell me that she had only been channeling for a short time, mostly for friends, and that she had only given a few private readings, the channeling process being quite new to her. It was clear to me that she was not overly confident, and when I asked her if her channeling work was going well, she replied that she is still going through a period of trying to be completely accepting and trusting of the process. She felt that it was a real growing process for her. She continued, telling me that sometimes she felt really confused, wondering why she was delving into channeling instead of pursuing a career or some more conventional way of earning a living. I told her that in my opinion, it would be a mistake to drop it now, and suggested that she accept what was happening, to trust it, to learn from it, and build on it.

RUSTY: Build on it for myself, you mean?

KIT: And for itself, too, build on the process. I mean for you as a learner.

RUSTY: Well, let's see who will come through. I'm going to give permission. My guides ask me if I will give permission for the extraterrestrials.

After about ten minutes or so of meditative silence, Rusty went into an altered state and another's voice came through her.

ALIEN: We use the sound to communicate to you our intentions of peace, love and of understanding. And we wish to express many wisdoms and beliefs which we carry at this time so that you may use them as tools to gather your people and together understand the transitions that are upon you. We are close by, within a 500-mile radius as we speak.

We wish to bring you a message of grouping. It is the belief and understanding we have used on our world to bring about the harmony and unity of our people. We have been to your planet before, to experiment with this belief often, and have met with much resistance. And the success of sharing our understanding has met many obstacles.

I have puzzled considerably about "grouping" as a concept and think it must refer to a communal way of living, which includes thought processes as a manner of influencing a way of life. If grouping is the foundation of their civilization's existence and explains the harmony and unity on their planet, I believe that we must try it. Surely if groups existed in large numbers here on our planet, groups whose members think alike, hold the same goals, ideals, share the same abhorrence of war and violence, the light encircling our planet would have far fewer "explosions" and far more of free flowing harmony. I wonder if this concept doesn't reflect the Christian idea of "if two or three are gathered together in my name, . . ." We are aware of the power of prayer, of coming together to increase our closeness to the Godhead, in theory, if not in practice.

ALIEN: We wish for you to understand the concept of light holding the energies for you to take and transfer into matter. It is possible to take the light that comes to your planet from what you call your sun—as well as the light that comes from a far distance that you do not recognize and often mistakenly call the "sun"—and transform it into matter or vibrations that may be used to soothe, to change emotional attitudes, to bring about calming effects, to raise the levels of health, and then also to use as the purest food source. It is a process that we have used and understood for a long time.

It is through the groupings that this transformation of light into matter or vibration occurs. It is when a grouping of persons within the same vibratory rate are together with concentrated purpose, not upon the self but upon one ideal or goal—a group consciousness—when the vibration comes into perfect alignment with each in the group, that then the light that has been contained can be brought within the group and the vibration focused in rays upon the light. Thus you may use it for the chosen purpose.

It is through this process that we are able to bring harmony to our planet, to make our people raise their consciousness and understanding of their own Godliness, to make their struggle of oneness easier and more complete. For, too, we have among us many teachers and masters with far greater understanding than we possess.

It is through this procedure of the grouping that we are then able to share with all in our homeland, the understanding. It was also then that we were able to feed our people when the lightstorms came and our food sources were destroyed. We come then at this time to teach and to share the grouping, the belief, with your people so that you may use it to bring about the calming effect when the fear runs rampant on your planet, when the hostilities and the hate, as you so call them, are everywhere and turn one upon one another. It is then that certain groupings will actually be able to bring about the calm.

It is also important to share with you the understanding of the food source of the light. Am I making myself perfectly clear?

KIT: On most things, yes, but I don't understand two things: I'm not sure about the groupings, and then I don't understand what you're telling me about the source of foodstuffs from the light.

ALIEN: It is when you take the light that penetrates your planet and it is allowed to be brought into receptacles that are built or made out of certain minerals that you will actually be able to hold the light. It is then when the conscious thought and the raising of the vibrations of certain groups that have worked so closely with each other that they are in perfect attunement, that they may take the light and transform it into an actual food substance that may be assimilated by the bodies you possess. Do you see?

The space being then continued offering instructions concerning the problems of our food sources when the earth's weather changes come. Since the pollution we have created destroys our sources of supply, it will be absolutely necessary for us to have alternative sources developed.

The alien voice spoke about their experiments at this time in bringing groups together, trying to line up individuals of the exact same vibratory level. I am told that much resistance has been experienced here on this planet and just now, according to the alien, scientists are being worked with, to communicate to them the understanding of the elements that must be used to build the containers needed for these purposes. Once this is understood, the alien continued, the light thus contained can be used for food, for building, for dissolving pollutants. They call it the Mother Light and use it for all that carries their life source.

When the Alien spoke of dissolving pollutants, I was reminded of the suggestion given me some time ago by Indira regarding this very subject—i.e. to interest scientists in the possibilities of neutralizing toxic pollutants, including atomic wastes, which I discussed in Chapter Seven. When the Alien spoke of using the light from the containers, the concept agreed completely with Indira's advice on using vibrations of the same frequency as the toxic wastes to neutralize them, thereby destroying their potency.

When I asked about the name of their planet, and if it is possible to express their beings, the alien told me that they come from far away, and it is only a knowing, a vibration they have, and that on their planet each being can merge with the others which gives them an understanding of everything about the other, including the consciousness. It is as if each of us, upon meeting with another human for the first time, would know instantaneously exactly who they are, what the other feels, their genetic composition, even including their spiritual growth. And, I suppose, there are a growing number of perceptive and enlightened people walking around these days who are capable of this kind of instantaneous "knowing."

I asked how to form groups capable of being of use in spreading this idea of "grouping" and was told that sounds are to be given to me to be spoken or sung together. If the group is in vibrational sync, we will experience simultaneously the turning on of bright light. The voice also told me that they will anticipate with much excitement the experiment and will be present to monitor the vibrations.

I tried the experiment soon after the session, with three friends, and although none of us felt the light, we all enjoyed the sitting together and chanting the words. The voice spoke of them as vibrations put into words for me to use. It is one line, with five sounds, repeated as often as wished:

HO BEE YA TA HO

The first sound is sung quite high, then the following three lower and more monotone-like, with the final word slightly higher, though not quite as high as the first.

These communications from extraterrestrial beings are a new phenomenon in my experience. For myself, I find no difficulty in accepting communication with space beings as a fact of life. No stranger than when I first began working with Verna Yater and having ongoing conversations with those on the other side of the veil, to quote Indira. That is now so entirely within my daily pattern of living, that I no longer think of it as phenomenal, although I am aware that people look at me strangely at times after they've asked what my book is about.

After the space being left, Godfrey returned and took control, speaking once more through Rusty. When I mentioned the entity I'd just communicated with, Godfrey corrected me saying that he wished to make it clear to me that the voice I had heard came not from an entity, but from an "actual living being, not unlike you yourself and your brothers and sisters on your planet here. They are going through a similar process as you are to come into more complete understanding of their godliness, of their oneness, of their "isness." This is why they desire to assist you and to communicate with you. It is part of their experience to try to share with you what they have learned."

I asked Godfrey if we are all on the same path, all seeking the same unity, and he says that we are all of the same oneness but that there are many parts of God that we do not completely understand or accept, and that we must go out and experience so that we may come to a greater understanding of our completeness as God.

GODFREY: It is a gift to be able to be in this reality, this dimension, to struggle, to laugh, to love, to hurt, that you may know one more part of the beautiful light that you are of God.

There are many parts of God that the soul that you are has already understood, and through your ability to serve others, to express love, to express understanding, you are able to understand more completely what it is that you are that makes up the God of which you are a part.

I told Godfrey that to increase my understanding was my dearest wish. He continued speaking, telling me that God is not a fixed entity, not a fixed understanding that once you come to it is suddenly all understood. God changes and expands and evolves as we do, for God is us and we are a part of God. As we change, so does God. It is a continuous process for all that are involved to come to this raising of our consciousness, this understanding of our godliness. It is never ending, but expands constantly into more love, more greatness. That is what God is, according to Godfrey.

KIT: That's a fascinating concept, that God expands as we do.

GODFREY: For you see, we are God. God cannot be complete without each one of us, which is why He has created us as we are. We are given the opportunity to evolve at our own rate, and so it is that as we evolve, so does God.

Godfrey went on to stress that I must be clear about the extra-terrestrials, that they are not the "perfect" aware beings above us, as humans might tend to think, looking down upon us and helping us. Like ourselves, the aliens are in the universe for their own particular experiences, and that those experiences and knowledges, to use one of Indira's phrases, are for sharing. Through the act of sharing, trust is created.

Godfrey believes that experiences on our planet are very brief, intense but brief. Our brothers and sisters on other planets have much longer experiences as well as less (emotionally) intense and more balanced lives. This is why they are fascinated with our particular planet. Their dream has been to bring about a more even reality, and they wish to experience the intensity of our emotions. And our dream has been to create this quickening, this intensity, that we may go through a much deeper understanding of our godliness. It is ideal for all beings to experience all other beings' dreams, all experiences that are theirs, though not all choose to do this.

I was of course interested in hearing that we do, indeed, dream our own realities, and was told that many of us have the ability to dream more than one dream simultaneously, and that we can even superimpose one dream upon another, thereby creating dual realities.

Godfrey then told me that my essence has decided to have two experiences at this time, simultaneously. It is as if I took a leg, he explains, and placed it here on earth to walk around and experience this particular reality, and at the same time, placed an arm upon another planet for it to have the same experience elsewhere. It is still part of my soul, living out different realities at the same time. According to what he told me, when the two consciousnesses are aligned and come into understanding at the same time, it is as if your energy, your essence, shoots up to a much grander light, a much grander consciousness of God. "It is like what you would call a *double whammy*," he said.

KIT: Would this explain the sharp little glimpses into other realities that I am experiencing?

GODFREY: Most certainly. At times, the reality slips in and out, and you must remember that you are part of the same consciousness, still the one energy, the one soul.

Our conversation then turned to the speed-up of the vibrations of this planet, as well as our own vibrations. I have certainly been aware of my vibrations being speeded up and of things happening to me and around me with much greater speed. Godfrey talked about animals, about the dramatic changes occurring within their habits, and within their seasonal cycles. Certain unusual migrations are now beginning on earth, and he warned that we must pay attention to what the animals do, that if it were up to us, the people of America, it seems we would eliminate them altogether except for having them in our freezers. Godfrey and I enjoyed a small laugh at his dark humor.

GODFREY: You see, the animals are actually beginning to gather. You will find that this indicates certain areas that will be safe for a time, as dramatic weather changes are soon to occur. I do not mean huge storms with floods, thunder, lightning and so on. I refer to drastic changes in temperature, enough to affect in a most hazardous manner, the flora and the creature life as well as the human life around it.

Everything is in a delicate balance, and when these changes begin, the nature of the people of this planet is that they do not change. They remain rigid. They will fight almost to the end to maintain what they feel is their home, their reality, what they believe is owed them, you might say.

But if you allow yourself to grow and change with the earth, you will find that you will become a part of it. There will always remain a balance upon this planet, always remain a flow of life. There is an energy that follows the planet. It is as if the energy collects and then shoots in a pattern, in a circular pattern around the planet. Your longitudes and latitudes were first conceived with the idea of being within the grids and the energy patterns but then lost complete sight of the purpose that they were designated for and now are no longer of importance as far as energy grids.

Godfrey says that much is going on *within* the earth itself, many changes, and there will be an exchange, as he puts it, of beings living within the earth. They will emerge and will share their beliefs and their culture with certain ones upon this earth. He says this will be soon. This will give us the opportunity for expansion, to truly understand how much more we are a part of. We are of the same genes as those within the earth but have chosen to experience another reality on this planet. The beings who will come have much to share with us, as we do with them. For one thing, it will help us to realize how limited our reality is. The beings from within have polished their beliefs, their skills, and brought them to a perfect understanding. Now they will share them with us.

I asked Godfrey now about the future of Santa Barbara, when these great earth changes come about. He replied that this area will undergo enormous changes, although the energy and the life force that exist here now will return and reconstruct themselves. He then told me not to worry, that each person will be exactly where it is that they have chosen to be for the exact experience they have chosen.

Godfrey also spoke about crystals buried in New Mexico which act as tremendous energy generators. According to what he told me, they absorb energy for extended periods of time and can then release them in one powerful blast. They absorb God energy, light energy, and have also been absorbing the pollutant energy and purifying it. It is here that the aliens, the extra-terrestrials, are able to come and renew their energy. Many of the crystals are not even buried underground, they are just not seen by humans.

I asked Godfrey about "ley lines," a phenomenon about which I've heard, though I've never had a satisfactory explanation on the subject.

GODFREY: It is as if there were magnetic areas upon your planet that draw the energy in particular areas. If you were to see your planet from above, you would find one here, one there, and so on, major drawing points where the energy is brought in, not only from the universe but from all light forces on the planet. It is from these energy points that the energy is then sent out in streams of a circular pattern. It is the life force of the planet itself.

When Godfrey spoke of these circular patterns, I thought immediately again of Teilhard de Chardin's 'Ring of Consciousness' encircling the earth and available for all to tap into.

Godfrey continued, telling me that although our scientists think of the core of our earth as being fiery hot, it is actually very cool and very bright, as if there were a sun in the center of the earth. It is a pulsating energy source and is connected to the grid patterns that dissect the planet and send the energy. These grid patterns light up, Godfrey continued, and can be seen from a far distance. It is what is used by extra-terrestrials to home in on. "If you were to be far out in space you would be able to see the energy grids circling around your planet," he explained.

He went on to say that our thoughts create energy that actually can take on colors, lightstreams that can be seen from a distance. When thoughts are in harmony there is a continuous flow of movement, and when hate, fear, greed and so on predominate, it is as if there are explosions of light, and the energy is fragmented.

According to Godfrey, I have been given this information regarding sitting with others of the same vibrations as mine, as a tool to use in seeking out those who have this compatibility. Until this is done, no work in expanded ideas will be able to be brought to the group. One powerful energy source may create one group thought.

When all come into harmony and unison, he continued, and a group thought is created, that thought can manifest as food, as energy which can be used to build buildings, transport people, create shelters from pollutants, from the highest to the lowest thought may be made manifest. This requires patience, which requires cooperation, which requires acceptance, which requires trust.

It is trusting each other to act in the most loving of ways to create this powerful group thought. It is what they are using on their planet where some disharmony now exists. They use this method to quiet the dissident ones, to completely submerge them in love and peace.

When I say that we are here to learn and serve our fellow beings, Godfrey says I must serve myself first, then to teach and thus serve all. He suggests telling others about this so that they may form their own groups thus widening the consciousness-raising groups world wide. In this manner, expanded ideas will mushroom all over the planet.

CHAPTER 10

Dolphins

STEVE AND I had an extraordinary experience recently. We were invited to be present when Barbara Rollinson, Verna's partner and co-founder of the Spiritual Sciences Institute, telepathically channeled the consciousness of a dolphin.

Having been addressed not long ago by an extraterrestrial, and now by a dolphin, the communication possibilities available throughout the universe are also mind-blowing. Underwater species as well as outer-space beings, all inter-communicating!

"I think, therefore I am," as the philosopher Descartes said long ago. The implicit assumption in that remark is that we alone of all of God's creatures, have the capacity to communicate. *How is it possible for mankind to be as arrogant as we are?*

When entering or leaving a foreign harbor I have often found myself thinking about the seagulls swooping and calling their shrill cries all around me. They have no trouble communicating with one another, the Peruvian ones with the Irish birds, or those in New York harbor. Strange, isn't it, that they can and we can't?

An article in the Los Angeles *Times*, May 22, 1986, carried the headline: "Elephants Seem to Excel at Chitchat," and told the story of two women zoologists who have demonstrated that elephants "do, in fact, communicate by infrasonic means—with sounds at frequencies too low to be detected by the human ear."

The article goes on to say that since the advent of highly-sophisticated audio technology, the zoologists have discovered that elephant "rumbles," which for years had been thought to be the sounds of their digestive tracts at work, "were often the upper harmonics of sounds unheard by the human ear. Moreover, the intensity of the sounds recorded suggest that they could carry to elephants for long distances. . .The theory, still unproved, that infrasonic elephant calls could carry as far as *one or two* miles, makes sense," the scientists, Moss and Poole, told reporters.

Again it is the situation of man's advancement in the areas of science and technology bringing a broader perspective of the world in which he lives. Just as the elephants can conceivably communicate across a two mile distance through harmonics, why shouldn't dolphins, whales, and all sea creatures in their liquid medium of the ocean, be able to communicate with one another across great distances?

Extending this train of thought further, although I acknowledge that we must stretch our minds considerably to admit the possibility of dolphins communicating telepathically and having their thoughts channeled into spoken English by a human medium, I have to ask once more: "*how do we know that it is not possible?*" Of course we don't, and there must be many thousands of people world-wide who have had communication with dolphins. Someone recently told me that only two creatures, it has been said, are "ensouled": humans and cetaceans. This may be so, yet I personally am inclined to believe in the ensoulment of all life.

Verna, Barbara, Steve and I met at the Santa Barbara Sound Studios for the recording session on a bright morning in June. Barbara had brought a mattress pad with her and spread it out on the floor inside the studio. Dan, the engineer, adjusted the microphones to the medium's prone position. Dan told us he'd had a lot of different experiences in his years as a professional sound technician, but the channeling of a dolphin through a human medium was going to be a first.

Prior to going into her self-induced trance condition, Barbara offered some introductory thoughts about the methodology of dolphin channeling itself:

BARBARA: Dolphin channeling is a two-aspect process. First, the transference of energy from the dolphins to myself is overlaid on my physical body. Unlike other trance channeling experiences, in order for me to channel dolphin energies, I must be lying down. It is a total body involvement, and the body responds by moving in an undulating manner.

Second, after that energy is in place, there is a telepathic or mind-to-mind transference of thought, and I then speak these transferred thoughts in our language. This telepathic communication makes it possible to speak with dolphins without being in their physical presence.

Many people have asked me, "Why does there need to be physical involvement to obtain the dolphin information since there is such a physical strain on my body?" The answer was given that it was a gift of energy for healing given by the dolphins. Otherwise, it would only be a telepathic transference of thought. . .

When all was set in place, microphones properly arranged, Barbara lay flat on her back on the mattress in front of the three of us, and her body appeared to become slightly rigid as it arched upwards. Her head was flung back, and from her mouth came a volley of high-pitched little shrieks, eerie, and definitely dolphin-like. As Barbara's entranced body moved, it made a soft, swishing sound on the sheet on which she lay, and the sound reminded me of the soft hissing of a wave spending itself on the beach. Her body then appeared to relax a bit, and almost immediately began an undulating movement, and, speaking in our tongue, relayed what she was getting from the dolphin. I must add, by the way, that through the entire forty-five minute dolphin channeling, Barbara's body never stopped its rhythmic undulations, nor did the meter of it ever vary from its slow, repetitive motion.

In answer to Verna's first question, the dolphin told us that her name was Yuka, and that she was, at that moment, swimming off one of the Hawaiian islands. She told us she was free, not in captivity.

Yuka went on to say that dolphins have existed on the planet in other, *lighter* forms since its inception and that they have also lived on other planets, in other forms. According to Yuka, Sirius, known to us as the Dog Star, as well as the planets known as the Pleiades, sometimes called the Seven Sisters, have also been home to dolphins. They are closest to the dolphins' vibrations, as well as to ours. When dolphins permit themselves to be captured, it is to help us, to teach us in loving ways, to be near to us while helping. I wondered about this, thinking about the whales and dolphins who have beached themselves as several have done recently on both coasts of this country. I feel both dolphins and whales to be gentle creatures, and it is vital for us to continue trying to communicate with them as they try to come to teach us.

I addressed Yuka, saying that recently an extra-terrestrial being (through a trance channel) had told me of their ability to know one another totally, in all ways, including spiritually, the instant they meet one another. I wanted to know if dolphins also possessed this ability. Yuka replied yes, adding that dolphins also traveled in space by telepathy, and today communicate easily and at will with beings from outer space. In this connection, when the extra-terrestrials visit our planet, according to her, they apparently travel underwater as well as through our skies.

That day in the sound studio, we were told of numerous ways in which we humans are now being helped by undersea creatures—softening the effects of underwater explosions, using electrical energies on the planet to permit harmonious energies to permeate Earth, as well as trying to detoxify some of the oceanic polluting energies made by man which now threaten us.

In reference to underwater explosions, Yuka told us that the sonic radiation emitted by human military underwater testing explosives does not dissipate in their watery environment, although it does lessen somewhat in time. This raises the possibility that the effect of those military experiments on our underwater brothers and sisters may destroy, or at least severely stress, their auditory faculties. Again, I can't help wondering if this might explain the many instances of whales and dolphins beaching themselves for "no apparent reason," as the scientists often tell us. Might it be that these underwater explosions cause a disorientation of their senses of direction, resulting in the mysterious beachings? Later that same night after the dolphin channeling at the sound studio, twenty-five small-sized whales beached themselves off the west coast of Florida.

YUKA: We are with you again and we give much thanks to the kind consideration that has been given to this channel and the transmissions of energy. We are here to help in whatever manner we may serve.

VERNA: Thank you very much for coming today. May we pose some questions?

YUKA: Yes.

VERNA: I wonder if you could give us some information about your special dimension and importance of your existence on the planet at this time?

YUKA: Our reason for being here is to be of service to those upon the land and in the sea. We hold that all being, whether they be in human form, animal form, in plant form, or in mineral form, are all of importance. And we are here to interact with each other. We're also here to demonstrate the importance of sound, noting that sound comes from the interweaving of transmissions of energies. And we help to keep that energy in a balanced form upon the sea. (*Yuka's comments reminded me of Indira saying that sound is the glue that holds the universe together.*)

YUKA: Much of electrical energies and sound is being polluted in the airwaves, as well as upon the land and the sea, and we are attempting to bring that into balance upon the seas. We also have the ability to communicate in a more holographic manner than you humans do, meaning that we perceive things as a *totality*—not simply through sound or through the visual acuities of eyesight. We help in this manner of giving ways to communicate to others and ways to see that indeed there is a deeper dimension of experience. To give information such as this is part of the reason we have been coming through such channels as this one.

VERNA: Could you speak a bit more on distortion of the sound waves and the oceans, please?

YUKA: It is not truly understood that when demolition is done, or explosions released under the sea, that those sounds *do not diminish*—the intensity of the blast diminishes, but not the continuation of the vibrations released by the detonations. It is always left in a vibrational form in the ocean itself.

VERNA: Is there anything that can be done to totally remove those vibrations which remain?

YUKA: No, once it is there, it is there. It is only changing the intensity which we are able to perform.

VERNA: Could you tell us also about any influence which you have about the moderation of sound distortion on the land?

YUKA: Only that it needs to be attended to.

Yuka continued, telling us that when certain sounds are produced, certain *unharmonious* sounds, whether created by human voice, mechanical devices, musical instruments or other, the consideration must always be, how does it affect the physical body? Some are beginning to understand this on a deeper level and are using, for instance, the harmonious sounds of music to better balance the physical body. But unfortunately, it is only a minority of humans who have this understanding.

VERNA: Do you have any other suggestions for us as to how to lessen the pollution of the atmosphere?

YUKA: One is to have all of your countries recognize the need for a continual concern. First, there has to be a recognition of the need and then comes the ability to do something about it. There is already technology available upon your land, but this question does not have the support of the individuals in order to put it out there.

If the governments of the world saw this need, laws would be passed prohibiting all pollution.

Verna asked Yuka what the technology might be and Yuka told us that first of all the vibrational forces of some of the machines must be altered. In other words, the pitch must be changed, the tone, the actual electrical energy as it comes through the machine so that it is of a healthful beneficial energy for the body, rather than being a harmful bombardment upon the physical self.

VERNA: Could you tell us something about the holographic way in which you utilize communications and in which you use the energies?

YUKA: We perceive things holographically. Whether we are in our natural habitat, or even when in captivity, we are constantly in communication with each other, as well as with those around us. It can be used in the form of sensing. In other words, if we are given an object, we not only sense the object's shape, but its total dimensions and where it came from as well.

Yuka continued communicating with us, speaking of earlier forms in earlier times, of other planets and said that when they permit themselves to be captured, it is to be of service to us in whatever way possible. She says that the dolphins are sometimes greatly distressed at the treatment they receive at the hands of humans, knowing that it is affecting the spiritual and karmic growth of the individual or individuals involved.

I asked Yuka if they are able to communicate entirely with other dolphins as if merging one into the other in the manner of the space beings, to know the others spiritually, as well as in all other dimensions, and she replied affirmatively. When questioned further by Verna she told us that she chose to communicate with us partly because of the willingness of the channel, Barbara, to give of herself, and also to send energies through her to us. She continued speaking of the dolphins' own guides, "those wise ones," she called them, and said they were with us at that moment although not physically. In addition, Yuka told us she speaks not only for herself, but for many.

I asked her if she was aware of any spiritual advancement of the human race, and this was her reply:

YUKA: Yes, there are many who come now to experience our vibrations as we are with them physically. There are also those who are becoming more telepathically attuned and are willing to send out our information as it comes to them. Yes, there is a quickening, an intensity and a change in the perception of your vibrations to a more positive and spiritual aspect.

I then wanted to know if this will help communication between the human race and the dolphins and was told that it will, and between humans themselves also.

Steve next asked the dolphin for information about the ruins of Atlantis, its locations and other information, and was told that it is not the time for release of that knowledge, not only about the ruins but about the vibrations that have been set up there. In the next two years, information will be provided for those with Atlantean past life experiences who are currently on this plane.

In answer to Verna's questions about the healing properties of the waters around the island of Bimini, Yuka replied that there has been a complete vibrational change in that area which has helped in clearing and cleansing. Those from other galaxies have helped in this changing. These waters can be used for their healing properties by bathing in them, and by holding some of the water in a small container, so as to benefit by the vibrations.

VERNA: Are there other areas of this planet as far as the oceans are concerned, that might be used in the years ahead?

Yuka told us that the coming years will bring the need for greater cleansing of the oceans. Now, she said, there is more pollution than there is benefit of healing.

At the moment, according to her, there are oceanic regions which the dolphins consider "dead areas," areas where there is no life, no energy, and such places will have to be replaced and recultivated. Yuka said that the dead areas have had high concentrations of pollution, not necessarily from outward sources, meaning dropping things into the sea, but simply by having such bad energies chemically, or electrically given that the living creatures stay far away from them. On the other hand, according to what she told us, there are particularly high energy fields around certain islands and coastal areas—the Bahamas, the Hawaiian Islands, Australia, as well as the western and eastern coasts of the United States.

KIT: What would you have us do that would most benefit this planet right now?

YUKA: The greatest benefit that you can give is the positive intent of communication through love, whether that love, that communication, is sent to another human, an animal or a plant. Giving back in a healing manner what is being taken from the earth, whether it is the sea, the land, or the atmosphere around you.

Steve asked if there is underwater communication between dolphins and extra-terrestrials and the answer was yes, not only in the water itself, but also telepathically, and also with others not of this galaxy.

These beings, according to the dolphin, come to seek ways of helping. They guide them as well, to areas of need and when necessary, give them a "shower of protection" to prevent detection by us. The dolphin described devices which pick up the forms and areas where fish and dolphins and other mammals live, a cosmic radar of sorts. Yuka explained that when the beings from outer space are swimming with them under water, they are protected from human detection by these devices. She said that they do not participate in space travel with the extraterrestrials, communicating when out of the water by telepathy only.

I asked Yuka what she would have us do to better working relationships between the dolphins and humans, and she responded by describing a great spiritual connection between humans and dolphins. She says that when there is a greater recognition that we are all interrelated upon the planet, that we are of them and they of us, as she says, there will be greater respect for taking care of all living things upon the planet.

YUKA: We have great respect for each other. Each one, regardless of age or sex, is given their own respect. There is much communication with the young ones in teaching them all of these areas of service, of giving to each other, and of helping wherever the help is needed.

We have a great sense of joyousness, of freedom and of companionship—always. We are with each other whether we are next to each other physically or not. So there is never loneliness, fear or anger, only the desire to help and protect each other.

When asked by Verna if there is any important knowledge that Yuka would want to impart, the reply came again that we must know that there is no separation between all living things, only a veil of misunderstanding or lack of knowledge. When love is surrounding there will *always* be communication. We wish to have great spiritual communication with you, and for you to know that we are always in the love force with you.

After a short pause, Barbara's body movements altered totally and her breathing changed as well. Deep sounds were heard and we were then addressed by one who identified himself only as a Great Whale. This being brought blessings, too, and love, and told us that the communication we were receiving from him was also being transmitted throughout the seas.

CHAPTER ELEVEN
Karmic Completion

IF I WERE GIVING ADVICE on how to handle the death of a loved one, family member, lover or friend, I would urge everyone to come to terms with that person, *before* the soul leaves the body, and most especially if there is unfinished karma between the two of you.

I unfortunately did not come anywhere near such a state of completion with my father, and only partially with my mother, although I know I made some improvement in resolving our joint karma.

Curiously, I didn't feel I had any specific problems to work on with my brother. Our relationship in this round was always a pleasant one, but I don't remember it as ever enlivened by exciting sparks of communication. I thought of him as a man unfulfilled in many ways, but as he wasn't a communicative man, I can't really pretend that I knew him inside. Our lives were so entirely different, as were our personalities, that if it had not been for the fact that we had spent our youthful years together, as brother and sister, our paths might never have crossed. I wonder how much of this holds true for many of you regarding your own siblings?

Since I originally wrote the above thoughts about my karmic connection to my brother Laurence, Indira has told me that he and I have incarnated together fairly often, and generally in close relationships. She said that in ways I wasn't aware of, he helped me to "unravel myself," which again, in Indira's language, relates directly to the image of the emerging butterfly unraveling the threads of its cocoon.

My friend Steve Diamond has just given me a thought which strikes me as valid. He suggests the possibility that the very fact of my mother's obvious preference for my brother was exactly the catalytic situation I needed to spark my becoming the rebel I did become. Perhaps I needed that challenge to strengthen my own soul, as well as to begin the process of my unraveling. And so, while in my first analysis, I felt that I had no real karmic connection with my brother, it seems to me now that our relationship might have been the catalyst needed for this butterfly to emerge from her cocoon.

My father developed syphilis when I was a small child, and at that time the disease was not only unmentionable but incurable as well. I was never told what his illness was, but it was clear to me that his brain was damaged, and as a result his behavior was unpredictable. I remember on the night before my wedding, the panic that I felt wondering what shape he would be in. Sober or drunk was my first worry. Sober enough he was, and our progression together up the long aisle of the cathedral, with my hand tucked under his arm, the long train of my wedding gown rustling softly along the floor behind us, was as dignified and proper as I could have wished.

My father did not play a large part in my life after my marriage, and, looking back on it, I realize that there was never any desire on my part to be with him. He was a kind, mild-mannered man, until the months just prior to his death. As everyone knew, his opinions were based on nothing more than his own feeling of the moment, and conversation with him was difficult. I always hoped he never realized how many people avoided him and ignored what he had to say. My memories of him are of a slender, quiet man, always on the edge of a group, even when it consisted of his own family.

I had been married to Ted for almost five years when my father died. He had been admitted some time before to Johns Hopkins Hospital in Baltimore, and late one afternoon my brother called to tell me that our mother had just been notified that my father's death was imminent. In a way, his admittance to the hospital had come about because of me, and for some years I had this awful feeling that I had caused my father's death.

My parents had gone to their summer home in the Tennessee mountains just outside of Chattanooga, and that summer when I arrived for a visit with my two year old son, I was shocked to find my father a totally changed man. From a kind, self-effacing person, he had, in a few weeks, become another personality. He had turned hostile, aggressive, demanding, all the qualities he had not shown before were now exhibited as his new person. He had recently taken the car, insisting on driving himself down the mountain without the chauffeur along, and as he had not driven in many years, the inevitable accident occurred. It wasn't serious, he was scratched up a bit, but no one else had been hurt, nor had the car been badly damaged. What was frightening to everyone, however, was the suddenness of his psycho-emotional change, and the uncertainty of the future.

After I had been there a day or two, I had a talk with my mother, telling her that it was obvious my father needed medical supervision. She seemed unable to think for herself and asked my advice. I suggested she call my eldest uncle, my father's older brother, and talk it over with him. As a result, it was decided to invite an old friend, our family doctor, in fact, to spend a weekend on the mountain, and he persuaded my poor father to accompany him up to Baltimore for treatment. He never left the hospital, and a few months later came the call from my brother.

The following morning, the three of us flew up to Atlanta where we changed to a small, single-engined plane to continue our trip to Baltimore, as there were no commercial flights available. That was a nightmare trip, not only because of the mixed emotions I had about my father, but also because the weather was terrible, and, to compound the misery, I had a fierce toothache which had begun to develop the preceding afternoon. As we bounced through the sky in that little plane, hour after hour, the thunder, lightning, and pelting rain were unceasing. We finally reached Baltimore sometime after mid-night, all of us exhausted.

On our arrival in Baltimore, we drove immediately to the hospital where we were expected and one of the dreadful pictures indelibly etched on my mind's eye is that of my father lying under that oxygen tent, seemingly already dead.

But he wasn't. The oxygen tent was removed and when this pitiful, skeleton-like man focused finally on my mother's face, he sat up, held out sticklike arms, and gave an unintelligible cry. There, at last, was something to hold on to, was what he was expressing, something beloved and familiar.

My father died within the next few hours, a release, it seemed to me, from a really difficult life. His karmic path had been a hard one and in a recent session with Indira, I was happy to learn from her of my father's present condition in spirit. He is surrounded by love, she reported, is growing and learning and no longer very interested in this planet of ours. He will, however, be waiting to greet me lovingly when I make the transition and go behind the veil.

During that particular trance session, Indira also told me that when my father made his transition, a close friend of his named George was waiting for him, and that George had given him much loving support on his arrival. I have no knowledge of George's identity, although I have an intuitive feeling that George may have been someone my father saw and talked with perhaps on daily basis. He might have been an attendant at the race track where my father liked to pass his afternoons, a shoeshine man maybe, a bartender, a tipster, who knows, but it is entirely possible that George was the person closest to my father throughout the last years of his life. I suspect that George must have been a man of compassion and loving understanding and I send him my blessings for the love he expressed for my father. It was evident to all concerned that my father had been considerably disoriented before he made the crossing, so he was in need of much loving assistance on reaching the next plane of existence.

I've always felt guilty about my father, guilty about never having been able to love him, guilty that so often I found him to be a source of embarrassment, and what made it worse was my sure knowledge that of my two parents, he was the one who really loved me. I cried at the small funeral service held in the living room of my parents' home, and afterwards, my mother told me that one of our friends had commented on how much I must have loved my father to have cried so bitterly. But I knew better. Or did I?

Ironically, my life would be "easier" now that my father was no longer around to embarrass me, and I could now anticipate as well the pleasurable fact of inheriting a considerable amount of money which was to color my life from then on. But I would have liked so much to have been able to work out the karma between us in this difficult life of his before he died. I did realize eventually that I was in no way responsible for my father's death, and that realization did release me from any further guilt.

I have at times felt a real resentment against my father, never having experienced a father in a truly supportive way, in spite of my awareness of his love for me. This has colored my relationships with men all through my life and I have felt anger towards him for denying me what could have been considered to be my right. When I see affectionate fathers displaying that love towards their little daughters, and even their grown daughters, I sometimes feel envy with a child's longing for that protective paternal loving care.

My mother, as can be gathered, was the one who didn't love me, and her love, of course, was what I yearned for. My older brother satisfied her every motherly instinct, it seemed, and there wasn't enough love to go round. She wasn't a very maternal woman, and it wasn't until she had been dead for a few years, and I began writing about her, that I began to understand my mother.

She had been, as a very young woman, saddled with a sick husband whom she had to nurse, playing father as well as mother to her two children, family planner, decision-maker, travel guide on family trips which were frequent and far-flung, besides leading a very social life in New Orleans with all the necessary entertaining involved, and, on top of it all, determined to pretend that nothing was wrong with her husband. Quite a juggling act and she did it well. She was attractive to men throughout her life and had a lover here and there, to my knowledge, and perhaps others whom I didn't know about, and it seems right to me that she should have experienced that fulfillment.

My mother had been the youngest of four, and her mother had been left a widow at a comparatively young age when my mother was three years old. Being an independent woman with an indomitable spirit, and having a large house with several servants, my grandmother took in boarders to augment her income. With the financial backing of friends, she opened and successfully ran a day school where many of the future prominent social and business leaders of New Orleans were educated. With all of this activity, she also raised, educated, and loved her own children.

New Orleans had what I believe was the first Opera House in the country, and probably had as well their own resident company. Often, I have heard my parents and my grandmother speaking of world-renowned singers performing there. I well remember my grandmother telling me of the generosity of wealthier relatives: "Aunt Nellie and Uncle John would send their carriage around with a note saying that the children and I could have their box at the opera for that night, and that the carriage would pick us up at half past seven." I can visualize the scene of getting the children rounded up and dressed, and everyone scrambling to do his or her homework first, with perhaps one or two having to miss the performance due to pressure of school work. As a result, my mother knew practically every opera by heart, having grown up with them from her earliest childhood and although the Opera House burned to the ground during my own childhood, I became familiar with many of them myself.

I remember reading the news of the Opera House fire over the shoulder of the passenger in the seat just ahead of me when I was on my way to school in the street car one morning. Though it may appear simplistic, being permitted the grown-up freedom of riding the streetcar instead of being driven in the family car represented a triumph and a turning point in my early life. After this occurred, other freedoms seemed to come along with it.

One year at school, for example, I lunched every single day on the same fare. I would visit the drug store on the corner where the streetcar stopped and buy some peanut candies. These delectables were shaped like peanuts and filled inside with peanut butter. When I got to school they went in my desk, and when lunch time came, I bought ice cream, potato chips and sometimes a pickle at the school cafeteria. It may sound dreadful, but it was sheer heaven. Sweet, sour, and salt, a great combination. I would study the menu offered for that day at school and when asked at home what I had eaten for lunch, I would glibly produce the names of some items I had seen on the blackboard. I was really living!

There was no love to waste between my mother and myself and had she not had a stroke some eighteen months before her actual end, I would most definitely have felt as guilty about her death as I had about my father's. In a sense you could say I was presented with the opportunity to balance out some of our mutual karma and I acted upon it.

I flew down to New Orleans while she was still in the hospital after she had her stroke, and when I got there I saw her lying in that narrow bed, totally immobilized except for her eyes, the only parts of her which appeared to be alive, eyes which seemed begging me to help her. In that instant, I forgave her everything she had ever done to me from my childhood on. Although she recovered and regained some of her mobility, her speech was always difficult to follow as a result, but the important thing was that we had forged some essential bond, and we had a pretty good working relationship from that time onward. I would fly to New Orleans every few weeks to see her and although she wasn't able to communicate much verbally, I would sit by her bed and more or less intuit what she was trying to articulate. When she died, I was ready to let her go and felt comfortable about the times we had together.

As my mother was a very attractive woman, she had several suitors, and some four years after my father's death she married one of them. The man she chose was of medium height, slender and with smooth, shining white hair. He came of Nordic ancestry and this heritage was reflected in my step-father's very white, almost delicate-looking skin. He was a most successful manufacturer and his main factory was situated in a small river town in central Ohio. Rolling green hills and three rivers meeting made for an attractive landscape. My mother would take frequent trips away from her new home in order to enjoy the theatre and music she was so fond of, but she was so completely devoted to my stepfather that wherever he was, that was where she wanted to be. My stepfather was a wonderful man and he and I understood one another far better than did my mother and myself.

He lived in a large dark house made of red brick, also dark, and he had no idea of changing anything in or about that house. Although my mother had never lived in a small town and did not really like the new house, they were so much in love that everything became bearable for her, and her life became a joy for the almost twenty years they had together before Dick died of a heart attack. My mother settled into a comfortable small town routine. His family became hers, and a more congenial loving group would have been hard to find. Dick was himself a widower with four children, all of whom were married and had children of their own, and all of them right down my mother's alley, as they say. One of Dick's daughters was even named Phoebe, a striking and unusual coincidence since it was my mother's name as well. Those years were wonderful for her and I was grateful that she was finally having the happy relationship so long denied her.

But a scene remains with me for which I have never managed to entirely forgive myself, even after all these years. It occurred after she had moved back to New Orleans after Dick's death and at the time I write of she had again been a widow for a

few years. She had come to California for a visit with us, and
this was the day she was to return to the south. My husband and
I were living in the Los Angeles area for a few weeks during the
racing season and the scene I now remember took place in the
house we were living in at the time. My mother was short, had
curly brown hair turned salt and pepper grey, brown-green eyes
and was a bit heavier than she might have been. I see her now,
dressed in a suitably dark dress for travel, with one of the perky
little hats she invariably wore sitting on top her curly hair. As
she didn't like flying, she was going home by train. We were
sitting in the living room talking somewhat nervously, as people
do, when waiting for a parting to occur.

Mother sat on the piano stool and I at the other end of the
room. My husband was at the race track, and as I was reluctant
to brave the rush hour Los Angeles downtown traffic, we were
waiting for a cab to take her to the train station. But take her,
not us, since I had selfishly decided not to even ride with her to
the train station. All of a sudden, as I looked at her, she
appeared so sad to me, so forlorn, and so miserable that my
heart went out to her, and I was seized by a strong impulse to go
over and sit next to her, put my arm around her with some
affectionate words. And yet I couldn't make myself do it. I
could only sit making meaningless conversation, hating myself
and helpless to change.

Indira has told me that my mother did love me, in spite of
my feeling otherwise, but since she didn't love me in the way I
wanted her to, it never seemed to satisfy me.

Believing that we choose our parents, choose them for the
lessons we need to learn—as they in turn permit us to be born
to them—I have thought often about how I came to be the child
of these two people. I know I have learned a certain kind of
strength, a certain resilience from my mother, and I wonder if
perhaps I didn't choose my parents and familial situation in
order to develop under conditions and aspects which enabled
me to become the woman I am. Certainly many of you, on
considering this concept of choosing your parents, have initially rejected the possibility—as I did myself—saying, "Oh *no*, I
would *never* have picked them!" And yet, on deeper analysis,

haven't they created certain "conditions" which have led to your own self-unfoldment?

Similarly, I also selected out of the men I might have chosen, two husbands who were never able to give me the psychological or emotional support which I had not had from my father, and which I needed so badly. But, again, the result was to increase my own strength and self-reliance. Ultimately, it was my role-model-mother whom I followed.

It is a terribly hard thing to lose a child and although it was not a surprise for me when my elder daughter Diana died last year, it is an event which seems totally out of place and is still hard for me to believe. Nature didn't intend it that way and although both my grandson Thomas, Diana's son, and I, had been expecting her death, had in fact been discussing the possibility that her death might be imminent, nevertheless when we were notified it was a tremendous shock. Even now, months after the event, it still crosses my mind occasionally to call her when something comes up that I know would have interested her.

When someone close to you dies—whether it is a child, a lover, spouse, parent, or simply a friend—it's always the little things that make you catch your breath. For example, Diana and I both shared a delight in daylight-saving time, with a corresponding gloom when we would return to standard time, and almost invariably one of us would call the other with some remark about it. We took several trips together in bygone days, one to Italy and Greece when she was between marriages, two or three times down to the Golden Door spa for a week of strenuous exercise, slimming food, and lots of laughs together. Not that she needed slimming as she had a lovely figure besides really beautiful legs, legs which I envied no end.

Diana was married three times, the first two husbands being considerably older than she was, making me think that she was looking for a father figure. As it had been for me, her father was not supportive and trying to please him was difficult, whether it involved a new hairdo, dress, or social behavior. It seemed to me as if his casual remarks to his daughters were too often critical: so much so, that I sometimes commented on it, asking if he couldn't change his attitude and compliment them occasionally. His reply was that if he didn't think anything complimentary he wasn't about to pretend that he did. This attitude might have some justification to it, except that it seemed he never did like anything about them, and I know that both my daughters reacted against this paternal disapproval throughout their lives.

An interesting fact, to me at any rate, is that for three generations on the maternal side of my family, an identical pattern has occurred. My mother's father died when she was three years old, my own father was ill all of my life, and my second husband, the father of my two daughters, was never very interested in his children. What strikes me is the realization that none of us had what might be thought of as a normal father in our lives.

After Diana's drinking became so bad, it was hard for me to be with her. Alcoholism has been such a major factor in my life, with so many of those close to me bearing that burden, that I almost panic if I have to be associated in any close way with an alcoholic. But just thinking about Diana and remembering all that we shared, good and bad, makes me teary. And most of all, thinking of the sad, terrible life she had makes me weep again for the pain she must have suffered. But while I grieve for her loss, at the same time I am grateful to have learned from Indira that Diana will never again have to bear the terrible burden of addiction as her lesson was learned in this lifetime. And I am grateful also for having been the one to have assisted her to take such a giant leap forward on her path. Since learning from spirit that we choose our parents, and that we, as parents also allow this particular soul to incarnate through us, the lesson is clear.

This morning, while sitting at my dressing table, I picked up a small pottery jar, three to four inches high, a Hopi jar. Thrust into it are two owl feathers and a porcupine quill, all given me by my dear friend of many years, Katy Peake. The little jar now also contains a small pinch of Diana's ashes. Holding it now, I am taken away on a long train of thought reaching back to my honeymoon with my second husband:

We spent six weeks in Hawaii, most of them on Waikiki, in large, windswept rooms overlooking the beach at the Royal Hawaiian, then isolated in beautifully landscaped gardens. We had a broad lanai where we would have breakfast while enjoying all that was happening below. They were like weeks in Paradise, both of us young and wildly in love. I suppose both of us thought our lives would be forever filled with fragrant flower leis and the soft sound of the blue-green Pacific waters rustling on the sand. I returned from these flower-filled weeks pregnant, which was a real surprise for me. I had talked of adopting another child during my first marriage, not wanting my son to be an only child and not having conceived again. But one of my grandmother's maids had assured me that what I needed was another man, and it turned out she was right—so Diana was born.

I remember taking Diana down to New Orleans when she was five years old. I wanted her to meet her great-grandmother while she was still alive. My mother reported that Grandmother thought Diana was adorable, but had such a vulnerable look about her that she was made a little sad by it. And that was true. All of her life Diana carried that look of "Please love me" with her.

And then I think of another time, when we lived in Scottsdale. My husband and I had been in Los Angeles for a few days at the races and I had brought back boxes filled with little dresses and sunsuits for Diana. Her nurse and I were trying them on her, exclaiming at each one how darling she looked in them. My mother, who was visiting, came into the room, telling me how spoiled Diana would be with all that praise, but as I believe in building people up, and she did look adorable, I saw no reason not to say so. The strange thing about this remembrance is recalling the low self-esteem in which Diana held herself. I always tried to build her up, in compensation for her father's doing the opposite, and certainly many people have low self-esteem, but over the years as she sank further and further into serious addiction, it became more and more impossible for her to like herself.

I remember vividly her ill-starred romance with the Korean War veteran. He was the first of her lovers to treat her with scorn and at times contempt, which seemed to be a pattern she demanded from the men in her life. We choose, not only our parents, but our character challenges as well, it seems to me, and Diana had chosen the role of victim. She was charming and loving, had many friends who truly loved her, was herself lovely looking with that slender body until her last years when the alcohol had done its work. But it was a sad life she lived, and my heart was often heavy for her sorrows.

When I move the little Hopi jar around, I can hear a tiny sound made by the small amount of ashes I saved after Diana's body was cremated. It creates for me a mystical bridge between the flower-scented honeymoon on the far off shores of the island of Oahu and this final, small reminder of my daughter. The spiritual nature of the Hopi Indian working on his reservation in northern Arizona who shaped the jar reached out to the love her father and I had for each other and bridged that distance of time and place. I think also of the joy I experienced so many years ago when I was first told that I had a daughter. I thought they were only telling me that because I had wanted one so badly. But it was true and that little daughter was to give me much happiness before her own sorrows overcame her strength and she became a victim of her addiction.

As it had been with my father, Diana's death was a release for me. No more worrying, wondering, imagining the pain, the humiliation she might be suffering. In that way, I could be glad for her and for her son and myself. I felt as if she had at last escaped, and when I was told by Indira that Diana's lesson had been learned, that never again would she have to incarnate with that burden of addiction, "those terrible cravings," as Indira had called them, I felt relief.

After her body was cremated, a few of us, her closest family and a few friends, entrusted her ashes to the sea, as we had done when John died. My Hopi friends, Fermina and Thomas Banyacya, came from Arizona and brought with them a prayer feather for Diana, just as they had when John's spirit had left his body. To be given a prayer feather is a very special honor, the feather having been prepared in the kiva in a sacred ceremony for eight days, and for me, it marked an expression of love among brothers and sisters. Fermina seems in a unique way to be my sister, and I think of her as such.

Thomas Banyacya performed a ceremony here at the house with the feathers, chanting the Hopi prayers while working the smoke from a small fire he had built on the stones of the patio. Afterwards, we went down to the waterfront where we boarded a fishing boat belonging to a friend of Diana's son. Several of us had brought flowers to scatter on the surface of the sea, and Thomas had given me cedar twigs to drop into the water, which I did. All was done, we felt, in a spirit which would have pleased her.

My last conversation with Diana was by telephone. She had called me and it was clear from the first word that she was very drunk. We talked briefly, then I told her it was too difficult for me to talk with her when she was drinking and that I was going to hang up and would talk to her later. She became indignant, insisting that she had not had a drink, then I said to her: "Diana, you don't want the truth from me. You only want me to call you and tell you how wonderful you are, and I think you are, but when you are drinking I can't talk to you."

We exchanged a few more words then I hung up. I didn't express anger, only that it was too hard for me to talk to her under those circumstances. This was only a day or two before her spirit left her body, and strangely, I didn't have any feeling of guilt about it. I felt quite good that I had spoken the truth finally, and I was glad because I had done it quietly, without emotion, and I had the feeling that Diana hadn't minded either. I wonder if I wasn't experiencing some of the relief she must have felt at finally being released from her condition.

At the first session I had with Indira after Diana's death, she began by saying, "we wish to speak today about the spirit who has just passed over to our side. . ." Indira then told a bit about how it was when Diana made her transition, and she said that Diana wanted me to know that I was not to worry about our last conversation, that she recognized it for the truth and was glad that I had said what I had.

I write these words because they may well help others in similar circumstances.

Another Hopi jar is on my dressing table and it contains a few ashes saved from the terrible time when we let my lover's cremated remains drift from the window of the little plane, down to the Pacific Ocean below.

Into this jar with John's ashes I have put two eagle feathers and a dried sprig of white sage. These were given me by a Chumash friend, and as John spent so much of his life working with and for Native Americans, it seems appropriate for them to be with him—just as I know Diana, who appreciated all birds as well as all animals, would like the quill and feathers.

After John's death, his daughter Tamar and son Steve, plus several of his colleagues arrived here in Santa Barbara and all stayed with me while we waited for the cremation to be complete. They all seemed to have the same attitude towards me, as none of us had ever met before the tragedy: it was as if they were thinking "What have you done to my friend?" Some of them told me this later, after we'd all gotten closer, but I was so numbed with grief at the time that it probably wouldn't have touched me to learn that my intuitive feelings were right.

We had chartered two small planes to fly us all over to Hopi, and we took with us a container with John's ashes in order to drop them over the Pacific once we were airborne. I was struck by Steve, John's son, who proceeded to recite snatches of extemporaneous poetry: I had only known one other person with this gift, and that had been Steve's father, John. I remarked on it after he had stopped speaking, and he just looked at me blankly, remarking that he hadn't any idea of what he'd just said.

In Santa Barbara, on the morning of his death, John and I had discussed our immediate future as it wasn't feasible to return to Hopi while the ground was still frozen. John had had a marvelous time plowing one of the main fields belonging to Fermina Banyacya where the corn would be planted and it was exciting for him to think of returning to help plant the corn itself. It was almost like a sacred duty in his mind, as well as the pleasure it would afford him. And in truth it is an honor to be permitted to participate in the planting, for the Hopi look upon that task as worthy of high ceremony. John was never to see that corn.

That field of the Banyacya family lies under a high cliff, the beginning of Third Mesa, and when we had finished here in Santa Barbara with the giving of John's ashes to the sea, we returned to Arizona and in that same cornfield I placed a small handful of his ashes, as did Tamar, his daughter. Some time the following year, I took an apple tree over to the reservation and it is planted on the edge of the field. Later, after my daughter Diana's death, Fermina told me that she had taken another apple tree up to the field and planted it near John's tree in Diana's memory.

I believe that my greatest growth has come about as a result of John's death. I didn't go under, although I was close at times. Instead, at last, I picked myself up and slowly started the long climb back to normalcy, gradually becoming stronger along the way. I had help, both on the inner and outer planes, and with that help I made it.

CHAPTER TWELVE

Future Vision:
The Gaia Spirit

IT SEEMS THAT INFORMATION is pouring in all the time, expanding our horizons and pushing further and further back what we once thought of as the boundaries of our knowledge. I now believe that there are no boundaries, except for the ones we create in our minds.

The experience with the channeling of the dolphin, Yuka, as described in Chapter Ten, has only added knowledge to what I had already gained from reading. All the world knows of John and Toni Lilly's work with these captivating cetaceans, and besides their groundbreaking research there are ever increasing numbers of other explorers into the unknown who are also writing of new findings.

In Chapter Ten I mentioned the recently discovered information on elephant communication and found that as our human technology continues to develop, more startling discoveries are coming to light about the communication amongst these benign giants. It appears that they, too, talk to one another and although the sounds are low and seemingly emanate from their stomachs, they travel through the atmosphere to surprising distances. This research is only in its inception but the possibilities of course, are mind-boggling.

It seems that if we members of the human race, are to develop as we were surely put here on this planet to do, we must

first come to terms with the realization that all life is interconnected, and that we must learn with no delay, to accept the idea
of inter-communication with all life forms. This to me, is the
essence of the *Gaia Spirit*.

As startling as it appeared to be when people first began
writing about the sensitivities of an apparently uncommunica-
tive plant, aren't we now accustomed to the idea that plants
have feelings, emotions, reactions? And don't many of us hold
sprightly conversations with favorite plants, flowers, trees, and
so on? It might seem crazy and it is certainly controversial, but
for my part, I surely do believe that all life is One. Carry that
thought one step further and we may find it not totally beyond
belief to consider, as millions do all over the planet, that inter-
species communication is a simple fact of life.

An interesting aspect of all the new knowledge, is that a
great deal of it is directly attributable to the new technocracy.
As much as I prefer humans to machines, I find myself
admitting that without computers many new findings would
never occur. Nothing, it appears, is too insignificant for a
computer to concern itself with—from space exploration to the
low rumblings in an elephant's stomach to the distances that the
sounds made by dolphins and whales can travel.

Could it be that the successions of our previous lifetimes
have been in preparation for finally coming to these truths?
This is quite possibly a tremendous leap in our evolutionary
process, this newly developing idea of communicating with
other forms of life besides our own. It may also be the first
hesitant step towards allowing ourselves undreamed-of joyous
expansion. We are possibly on the threshold of allowing all
varieties of luminous beings into our own lives.

Having lived on this planet since the early part of the
twentieth century, it is easy to realize the changes I have
witnessed. What would have been called a miracle, not even
conceived of as a possibility when I was young, is now
commonplace. And the vast horizons which are now daily being
pushed back are showing us realities which appear dazzling to

our late Twentieth Century. No doubt these will be common-place to those who follow us a century from now.

Consider only the law of aerodynamics. That law has always existed but was only "discovered" by man in recent times, and now flying around the sky is an ordinary experience for many of us. We think nothing of how impossible it must have seemed before the first man considered such a weird concept.

The time when we will think of space travel as equally commonplace is not far off. It will be no unusual occurrence for all of us to have equal opportunities to be astronauts ourselves, I imagine. And after awhile it will be, "Bye bye darling, I'm off to Aldebaran today, back tonight probably, but better not wait dinner."

Depending on the ages of my readers, I can ask how you feel about snatching invisible waves from the air and producing intelligible sounds? For many it is such an accepted phenome-non that they will wonder why I ask the question. But there are some of us still around who remember a time when not only was there no television but radio was in such a stage of infancy that we accepted as inevitable the crackling static interfering with our reception and resigned ourselves to this handicap to our enjoyment of the new discovery.

I can hardly believe how much I have learned, and how far I have travelled in the past three years. I even seem to have acquired a grasp on the subject of physics, for example, as it has seeped into my consciousness in various ways, inspiring me to buy books on the subject. I remember one day seeing a book about crystals in the window of a bookstore dedicated entirely to metaphysics. I was only beginning to develop an interest in crystals, so I went in, bought the book, but my eye was taken with another book near it, *Mysticism and The New Physics*, by Michael Talbot. Intuitively, I realized that it was the real reason I'd gone into that store.

Since the coming shift of the earth seems to be so inextricably linked with the future spiritualization of human consciousness, I have begun reading a number of books on planetary changes, and prominent among them has been Jeffrey Goodman's *We Are The Earthquake Generation* (A.R.E. Press, 1978). I was amazed at how much the following quotation from Goodman's thought-provoking book reflects much of the information received through Indira and other spirit entities: "Cayce and my psychic group," Goodman writes, "feel that the biggest change the earthquake generation will experience will be spiritual—not in the form of organized religion, but in awareness, attitude, and concern for others. In a life reading for a friend of mine, Abrahamsen (a channel) talks about veils being lifted from people's minds during this period. As these veils are lifted, people will understand better who they are, where they have come from, and what their fundamental spiritual nature is.

"An entirely new vibrational environment is projected for the earth. In addition to the spiritual changes people initiate, they will become more spiritually aware as a result of the geological changes foreseen to occur because these changes eventually will establish a more harmonious vibrational environment to live in. The earth will undergo a self-cleansing process to overcome the distorted vibrations that man, through his free will has created over the centuries."

This correlates, incidentally, with the Hopi Prophecy of a time of Great Cleansing, and it also clearly reflects Yuka the dolphin's thoughts about the negative vibrations with which mankind has so blindly been polluting the earth's oceans.

"The psychics believe," Goodman goes on to say, "that nothing happens by chance, and that the survivors will have the opportunity for spiritual growth. The survivors will learn to give thanks in the midst of catastrophe. The greatest growth will come to the children as they learn to believe in the presence of God and to contact "higher" sources of information and guidance. But the psychics note that humanity will have to learn how to stop enslaving itself by its own laws.

"They say that humanity will have to learn to make practical use of all the knowledge it has accumulated and the resources it has been given. According to the psychics, since the

United States in particular has not done well in these areas, and has not cared for all those in need, it will undergo the various destructions foreseen and thus will have the opportunity to learn how to handle fewer resources."

It has long seemed to me as if we are following directly in the footsteps of the Roman Empire. Life among the affluent as shown us on T.V., therefore available for most of us to see, becomes more and more unbelievable. Recently I was watching a cooking demonstration on television and was appalled to hear the chef tell us as he placed the finishing touches on his dish, that nowadays it is the 'in' thing to serve two kinds of caviar rather than just the best Iranian, Russian, or whatever is in style at the moment. Must be great fun for those who have trouble having anything on the table to watch these aspects of the lifestyles of the rich and famous on their television sets. . .

I was reminded of an incident years ago when my husband and I were being guided through the Roman Forum. The guide was showing us details in construction methods, and pointed out how the bricks were laid in the last years of the powerful Roman Empire. They were smaller, with more mortar between them, placed carelessly as if done in haste with little thought for their appearance, and so on. That little talk has remained with me all this time, and has often been in my mind when I see extravagant waste everywhere as today.

No one seems to care now, and it has become commonplace to have cars recalled for defects in their construction, planes ditto, with both having disastrous results for the innocent among us who trusted our industrial leaders not only to know what they were doing, but to have integrity as well. What are we to think now, since the recent space shuttle disaster? No one seems able to place blame or to take it. Something is wrong, there seems no doubt about that.

My picture of life after the earth shift is based partly upon information I have received from spirit, and partly on my own desires for the human race. It is predicted that we will again, as I have written elsewhere, be in the position of having to be self-reliant, of caring for one another, of sharing our lives, our talents, of giving of ourselves for the benefit of all. We will live on the gifts our Mother/Sister the Earth will give us—seeds, vegetables, herbs—and it will be up to us to give her the care she will need to provide us with this life-giving sustenance.

The more I learn of the way of life of the Essenes, the more I see it as enriching, empowering, a life to encourage growth. They shared their teachings in their travels, and sought out the learning of those they encountered. They were peaceful people, scholarly in their pursuits, and believed in sharing openly with those in need. I like the sound of it and think it would be a fine life for the survivors of the shift.

In the *Earthquake Generation*, Goodman writes: "What can be expected in this new order of things, the Millenium that is supposed to follow Christ's return? Cayce said that we should all pray to be incarnated during this time. But this golden age is not supposed to happen instantly. It will take several hundred years to develop fully. I asked Abrahamsen to give me a brief account of specific changes. He told me that government, instead of regulating people, would put its emphasis on helping people to develop and regulate themselves." *This sounds like the emerging 'empower the people' movements now popular with those working for social change.*

"Mind-to-mind communication will be commonplace. While transportation will still be dominated by the airplane, there will be some teleportation, as in "Star Trek.""

"Education will teach people how to tap their inner power. Agriculture will use prayer to control crops and rainfall. The sun and the earth's electromagnetic field will be the main sources of energy. . ."

The Hopi Indians today still use prayer to control crops and rainfall. Their dances are performed for the sole purpose of bringing rain. All of their elaborate ceremonies, the splendor of the costumes (always in pristine condition), these are all for that purpose alone, to beseech the Great Spirit to give them the blessing of rain for their crops. It is fascinating to me to reflect on this and to remember that this has been their way of life for some thirty thousand years. A successful way, I may add, although a way that means a life of hard, never-ending work for both men and women.

I have been told by spirit that before this century is finished we will again understand the powers of the crystal as they were known and used long ago in connection with the electromagnetic earth forces.

It *was developed to really high-tech uses in Atlantis and was the sole source of power. Along with this information I was told that we will also regain the knowledge of dematerialization and rematerialization. This knowledge has always been possessed by the advanced yogis and adepts in the Far East, has never indeed been lost to them, and is said to have been taught by these adepts to Jesus, during the eighteen years he is thought to have spent traveling in Egypt, India and other lands. It may have been this yogic knowledge that he used when he arose from the tomb and was seen afterwards walking among the living.*

The Bible makes no mention of the "The lost years of Jesus," although numerous scholarly books have been written on the subject, and as a result many are not aware of this part of Jesus' life. I myself had not heard of it until fairly recently. History tells us that there were well-traveled trade routes all through the Middle East, so it seems logical that Jesus would have traveled to other lands, both teaching and acquiring new knowledge, as was the way of the Essenes.

I have had the extraordinary experience of being spoken to by the master Jesus. I say "spoken to" as opposed to "speaking with," for although I have been addressed by him five times through the channel, he has never invited me to ask questions, as have the other spirits who come through Verna. The last time he appeared he told me that although men thought that he had performed miracles all throughout his life, the fact was that it was only in the final three years of his life that he did so and that was after his return from these travels to the East.

Going back to Jeffrey Goodman's We Are The Earthquake Generation: "Psychics will be used to guide successful research. Medicine will rely heavily on healing via color, (Indira says the same) often with dramatic results. Cancer will be cured. There will even be limb regeneration. Crystals are also supposed to be used for healing and energy.

"Taking a long range view, it seems that despite the threat of disaster from cataclysms, the earthquake generation has a great deal to look forward to. . ."

On Aug. 27, 1984, I had a session with Verna during which Mother Mary came to speak with me, the first and only time that happened:

MOTHER MARY: I am Mother Mary, and the decision was made for me to come first on this day. I wish to talk about the qualities of nurturing and to show all who are upon the earth plane that the balancing of what you call the yin/yang energies is of necessity to bring forth the Mother.

We do not mean it in the literal sense. We mean it in the sense of providing that which is of life-giving quality, not to harm oneself, nor each other, and not to harm the planet itself. The planet you walk upon is as Mother to you, although you do not always treat it as you should your Mother. I have come to tell you that although I was known as the Mother of the Master Jesus, I am also His twin, His twin in the creation of all time. We have come through many centuries of being together. It is not I who put myself forth in this manner, it comes from beyond to show you the balance that must exist for those who serve.

Although my Son was among those who attempted to show the equality of the bodies, it does not matter whether you come as a man or as a woman in an incarnation. It matters only insofar as you have selected certain things to be done upon a particular path, for the spirit is the same. The spirit which has chosen its body is the only importance to be considered.

When this knowingness exists, that the body is only a covering of the spirit, then you will find the harmonies returning. This understanding will also lead to harmonies within the family. It will be understood then that each member is important. It matters not whether each work upon the aspects of the outer world, or upon the production of these things you term professions. It matters not. What matters is that there be caring for one another, that there be equality, the understanding that in spirit all is equal. There is no superior. All must work towards their own soul growth, their own understanding of moving toward God. In this there must be assistance, there must be helping each other to move forward on the path. But ultimately, each of us stands alone, for although much is written at this time of working together, yet in this togetherness, there must also be the recognition that it is always the individual, and only the individual, that must take the responsibility for his or her own soul growth. This cannot be emphasized too strongly.

I will stay for a bit of questioning for I do not come frequently but wished to address you on this day.

KIT: Thank you, Mother Mary. I am honored that you speak to me. I would like to know how best I can serve in giving out your thoughts.

MOTHER MARY: It is not you alone that must give this information. It is important that many must begin to learn, to understand. In whatever way you see fit, speak of these understandings to those that cross your path, those to whom you write, in all ways that you choose.

When you speak of the compassion of spirit, when you write of it, when you demonstrate it with your own actions, you are giving others the permission to do the same. It must be done within the hearts of all for the opening of the heart's center is taking place at this time.

If each one of us accepted this truth, which many say they do, that we are each a part of God, how could there not be compassion? How could we bypass the needy, the hungry, and so on, without being aware that we are bypassing God? Some day we will have this awareness perhaps.

My Son, too, worked upon this, not only for Himself but for those that surrounded Him. Again, it is the opening of the heart's center within the bodies of men and women that we stress and this must be very clearly understood.

The understanding is already deep within each of you, and so perhaps one of your tasks will be to remove the veils which are preventing those upon the earth plane from understanding these particular precepts. You can only do this word upon word, idea upon idea. You will also demonstrate along with others, those in both masculine and feminine form, that there is indeed the necessity to bring about the understanding now that in spirit all is the same.

So it is to show through demonstration, through the written word, through the spoken word. You cannot reach all in the same manner. My Son undertook to speak to many, and traveled countless miles to reach the people for this was the only method that was used at that time. The spirit is the same as when He walked upon the earth, but now there are opportunities to use different devices which were not available when my Son was here.

There is a revitalization of the spiritual search, as there is each time when a crisis is upon your planet. This quickening of the energies creates most unusual opportunities for all upon your earth at this time.

It is only to remind you that when my Son and I walked upon the earth it was a time of great opportunities. The human race tends to forget, but the cycle of history repeats and once again opportunities are created. This time is again a time of rare opportunity.

"Many will understand, many will not. Do not fret at those who do not appear to understand as you and others speak the words. Even when my Son was speaking, even when He was manifesting much of the glory of God as the Christed One during the last three years of His life, there were those who did not believe. So do not fret.

KIT: I am thinking what a gift I have been given to be living in this time of increasing opportunity.

MOTHER MARY: It will increase, even more. There is a tremendous surge of energy in every part of your planet and many people everywhere are beginning to have an inner understanding of the momentous earth changes occurring. New horizons are opening for many upon your earth plane.

KIT: Are you speaking of the earth shift?

MOTHER MARY: It is in indirectness that I am speaking of this because what you call the shift is not the most important aspect perhaps to concentrate on. It is the shift in energies, the shift in the actual speeding up of your inner urges, your sense of needing to reawaken your spiritual searching. Not all understand this, but a rapidly growing number of people do. This is what I speak of most clearly, most deeply.

KIT: On the afternoons when people gather at my house to talk, it is my hope that by the interactions between us, some of the veils will come off and we will be more open to see the spirit shining beyond the veils.

MOTHER MARY: Many upon your planet have become jaded and their hearts are not open to spirit. You must reach their hearts, and help them to open to the knowledge that they are God, each a small part of the God Force and that the loving and the caring are all there for each to experience. For those who live more in their minds, you must show how to meld heart and mind together. For when you do this, you will find that there is the greater appreciation, the greater knowing that in the long run, as you say upon your planet, they will not be able to move away from God.

That is a powerful message and I find myself awed even by being addressed by Mother Mary, as needless to say I have been on the occasions when her Son, the Master Jesus, speaks. There are extraordinary vibrations in the room after Jesus has spoken. I know it sounds strange, but the room is filled with peaceful repose. It was quiet before, but now it is a different kind of quiet, as if the universe itself has paused and there is only light and softness in the atmosphere. I imagine that to be addressed by any of the Great Masters, Buddha for example, would create a similar feeling.

Some time ago, I sat in a small room with some thirty others waiting for His Holiness the Dalai Lama. After a time I began to be aware of vibrations which I can only describe as holy. I glanced down the row of chairs and saw, a few seats away from me, a Japanese monk, a small man, completely surrounded by his own peaceful vibrations. He was a most humble man, dressed in a plain brown robe, and spoke to no one as we all waited. Whoever he was, he was a most advanced soul and though I have nothing but admiration and love for the Dalai Lama, and felt it a privilege to be able to be in that room, it was the Japanese monk I remember and wonder about.

It seems to me as if every now and then we come into contact, as I did on that day, with a particularly shining aspect of the God Force, and awesomeness fills the space.

A FEW NOTES ABOUT THE AUTHOR

MY FIRST FEW YEARS were spent in southwestern Louisiana along the banks of the Atchafalaya River, a slowly meandering bayou, sometimes choked by lavender water hyacinths and always inhabited by alligators and water snakes. It was a lovely place of sunlight, flowers and ancient oaks whose spreading branches could have sheltered everyone I knew.

With the exception of two years spent in Europe, we lived in the country until I was seven, when we moved to New Orleans. During the first few months of living in the city I experienced two events which were to change my life. The first one involved the grandson of our dear and talented cook. She had asked my mother for permission to have her grandson live with her during the school year. As he was similar in age to my brother and myself, we were delighted with our ready-made playmate. There was, however, something mysterious about our relationship which I could never understand. Joseph was never allowed to penetrate the unknown facets of our house any further than the kitchen and pantry. Never was he to see the horrid, heavy, red-velvet drapes falling to the floor, and certainly never was he to climb the stairs to our more intimate living spaces. The notion of integration had not yet entered the consciousness of the South, and when I asked my mother why skin color made a difference, I never thought I was given a satisfactory reply . . . but I became aware of what we now call a social conscience.

The next memorable event came one afternoon when, on returning from school, I strolled down the street to join a group of children skipping rope. As I approached, the girl jumping rope began singing out a chant to the effect that my grandfather was a millionaire. I was shattered. Although I hadn't any idea what she was talking about, I knew it was something bad, and right then began my feeling of guilt about being rich. I was deeply wounded by what was doubtless a

215

thoughtless taunt, but it was many years before I was able to understand the concept of stewardship and to feel comfortable about money.

After I had separated from my second husband, I immediately sought out, and was sought out by, people with like interests. I changed my lifestyle completely. I no longer attended large parties, which I had never enjoyed. I no longer went near the race track, even when one of our race horses was running. I gave most of my clothes away and wore jeans and sweaters. I rarely saw any of the people I had known previously. Living alone, free to choose my own life, was just what I needed, desperately. My time became occupied with political activities and social causes, and as I progressed along my self-determined path, I became increasingly aware of my need for spiritual study. I attended seminars, lectures, workshops, read books, talked to people, all the while deepening my spiritual involvement and evolution.

When I began working with Verna Yater, a new world—literally—was opened to me. Much of what I now have integrated into my self is a direct result of my involvement with the wisdom of the teachers in spirit whom I have come to "know" through Verna's channelling. Indira Latari, my Hindu spirit teacher, has made me aware that we are sent to this plane to do two things: The first is to learn to know and to love ourselves; the second is to learn to know and to love God. "All else," she says, "is extraneous," and the second will not be done until the first is mastered.